Deepak Bajaj is an ace motivational speaker, high performance coach, social media influencer, and #1 bestselling author.

Deepak was regional manager with an MNC when he set up a part-time direct selling venture in 2007. Within three months, he resigned his job to dedicatedly build and nurture his ever-growing business empire in record time.

Deepak's book, *Be a Network Marketing Millionaire*, is one of the most read and recommended books in the network marketing industry. It has been translated in 6 languages so far and is considered to be the most definitive guide book for every direct seller. Deepak has trained more than 7 lakh people in the past 16 years. His videos get millions of views from 100+ countries.

His live workshops and online courses are famous for bringing about instant change and lasting transformation. He has been featured in various magazines and has received the Best Debut Author of 2018 award. He is a regular keynote speaker at various events and is looked upon as the lighthouse of the direct selling industry.

Today, with more than a decade's experience in the business, Deepak Bajaj has become a brand unto himself, garnering iconic stature in the direct selling industry. Deepak's life mission is to empower people to live their dreams, and he accomplishes this by training people using the same tools and techniques that brought about his own massive success along with lakhs of other people for so many years.

Follow him on all major social media platforms and www.deepakbajaj.biz.

ACHIEVE MORE, SUCCEED FASTER

31 Hidden Benefits of Direct Selling
to Live Your Dream Life

DEEPAK BAJAJ

Manjul Publishing House

First published in India by

Manjul Publishing House

•7/32, Ansari Road, Daryaganj, New Delhi 110 002 – India
Website: www.manjulindia.com

Registered Office:
• 10, Nishat Colony, Bhopal 462 003 – India

This edition first published in 2020
Second impression 2020

ISBN 978-93-89647-35-8

Cover design by Bhavi Mehta

Printed and bound in India by Thomson Press (India) Ltd.

Dedication

This book is dedicated to you.

I know you have dreams and you are committed to do everything it takes to make those dreams a reality. I want to support you in your journey towards fulfilling your dreams through this book. This book will not only ignite your spirit to do more and be more, but will also serve as a toolkit that gives you inspiration, ideas and solutions.

The rules of success have changed over time. This book is a personal transformation tool designed to prepare you for massive success in the new economy and in the years to come.

Growing up in a village, studying in local schools, facing financial struggles, moving from a job to entrepreneurship, making mistakes and starting all over again from zero...I have been through all of it and I know how it feels. Trust me, every legend was once a beginner. This book is my salute to the legend in you.

Now is your time to rise.
Go for your dreams.
Stay unstoppable.

Introduction to this new revised edition

What you hold in your hands is the improved and updated version of the number one bestselling book in network marketing/direct selling industry. People working in all different companies with different products and income plans have multiplied their incomes and have grown their business many times with this book. All successful teams are using this book as an essential guidebook and building large business empires using the principles and tools given in this book.

New chapters and new tools have been added in this book because I want to see my readers at the top, living their dreams and becoming top achievers of their company in record time.

I believe time is the most important resource in a person's life and this book is my attempt to save at least 6-8 precious years of your life. I have worked in network marketing with my heart and soul for more than 12 years. I have created new records of income and achievement and created thousands of achievers using the same principles, tools and techniques that are there in this book in your hands now.

Now is your time.

This is your moment.

Follow the success system given in this book.

Give this book to all your teammates.

And don't stop till you reach the top.

I am with you.

Your success partner,
Deepak Bajaj

WHAT READERS SAID ABOUT DEEPAK'S LAST BOOK

Every direct seller and those who target becoming a millionaire should read this book.

–Kailash Bhattad, CEO, Mi Lifestyle Marketing Global Private Limited

One of the best books on how to achieve big in network marketing. It's a perfect gift for teammates to make them serious in business.

–Mubeen Muhammad

This book is like [the] Geeta or [the] Quran of network marketing.

–Dr Akhtar Khanwala

Amazing book for beginners, doers, experts and trainers.

–Pradeep Choudhery

Awesome book on how an ordinary human can become extraordinary.

–Nishant Choudhary

Everyday reference book to meet goals and life skills.

–Payal Kothari

This one book is enough for success in direct selling.

–Mukesh Singh

I have become unstoppable. I got ten years ahead with this great book.

–Lomesh Choudhary

This book will help all those people who really want to do something in life.

–Mahendra Singh Rawat

I got answers to all my questions. It will give rocket speed to my business.

–Nitu Jindal

This book is very important for those who want to fulfil their dreams.

–Mayur Patil

[Most] amazing book I have ever read in my life. This book changed my thinking. I have become a totally different person after reading this book. I will be a millionaire.

–Alka P.

This book is the Bible, Bhagavad Gita and Quran of network marketing. Need no other book to follow after reading this book.

–Arun Singh

Best ever book on network marketing

–Chintan Arora

This is the book that can change the life of all and can fulfil the dreams of people who dream of becoming rich.

–Harshada Nikam

Excellent book. Highly recommended. Such appropriate and structured content in every page of this book.

–Gaurav Mehra

One-stop solution for network marketing. Strongly recommended for those who want to avoid mistakes and achieve success faster.

–Vijay Tetarwal

Great book for new distributors as well as leaders.

–Rajesh Yadav

Any new person can easily achieve his goals by learning from this book.

–Neha Rana

This book is as sacred as the Gita. It's a guide for those who are seeking success.

–Himangi

WARNING

This book may inspire you to dream bigger.

You will get inspiration, ideas, tools and solutions that can change the game of your life forever.

This book may totally change the way you think, the way you look at the world and the way you work.

This book may move you to start taking action. Read at your own risk.

WHY SHOULD YOU READ THIS BOOK?

Twenty years from now you will be more disappointed by the things that you didn't do than by the ones you did. So sail away from the safe harbour. Explore. Dream. Discover.

–Mark Twain

May 2006 – I was a highly paid senior manager with a leading MNC when someone introduced me to direct selling for the first time. Being too busy and super successful in my career, I ignored him. But he kept approaching me and shared several success stories whenever he got a chance. In June 2007, after thirteen months of being repeatedly refused, he finally persuaded me to attend one event.

I had never before seen anything like it. Honestly speaking, I was shocked. I couldn't believe the extraordinary achievements of some of the ordinary looking people there. But I was puzzled after the event. There were two voices in my head.

1. The first voice wanted me to jump into the business right away and told me this was one opportunity that could fulfil all my dreams. Even in my sleep, I began seeing the faces of those achievers I had seen on stage, and I would wonder—If they could do it, why not me?

2. The second voice stopped me from venturing further. It raised doubts and concerns. How could it be possible? These people were lying, it said. Stay away. Focus on your job. Work hard for your next promotion.

That was a tough time for me. I couldn't ignore the call of direct selling, yet at the same time, I couldn't do it. One day, I would feel this is the best thing on earth and the next day, I would feel that is far from the truth. After meeting senior leaders and attending seminars in the field, I used to feel inspired but at my next presentation, my friends used to instantly shut me up with their logical reasoning and examples. A week went by, and I finally decided to start the business, even though those voices kept haunting me.

I would start the day with high energy levels, and after two to four meetings, I would grow depressed. Here are some of the questions and doubts that bothered me everyday:

- Is it really a stable business or career?
- Would it spoil my reputation and relationships?
- Can a shy and introverted person like me build this business?
- How can this business produce so many millionaires?
- Why do so many people fail in this business?
- Why do so many people talk negatively about this business?
- Is it easy or not?
- Will I get respect and social status after doing this business?
- Is it sustainable and can it really be passed on to coming generations?
- Can we really build a big business working part-time?

And many more…

Almost every night, I thought of quitting the business. But what kept me going was this one thought—quitting this business is always easy; in fact, there is nothing called quitting here. You stop attending meetings or stop communicating with the upline/team, and it will be assumed that you have quit. The other thought that roused my curiosity was this—if so many people are passionately building this business, there must be something they know which I don't know. Before I quit, let me fully understand what I am quitting. This put me on a quest to deeply understand the business. I believe the best way to understand something is by doing it, so I continued doing it with all my faith.

As I started building the business, gradually, my belief in the business and what it can do for a person's life got strengthened. As my faith grew, so did my achievements. I slowly realized that the problem was not the business, but my mindset. I was judging the business based on my past experiences as well as on my opinions and those of people around me.

I made the mistake of taking things casually and doubting the business for thirteen months. Today, when I look back, I feel that was one of the biggest losses of my life. I lost thirteen months because there wasn't enough correct information available for me to make the right decision. The only thing available was people's opinions. I want to save you from making the mistakes I did.

As of 2020, when this book is being released, I have literally lived direct selling for close to 13 years, and in these 4500+ days, I have given my heart and soul to this business every single day. I have seen a lot of ups and downs. Companies starting and shutting down, governments changing, regulations and statutory frameworks getting stronger, people's opinions shifting, different phases of the industry, changing styles of working, teams being built at rocket speed and then crashing in no time. All my experience of learning from the world's best direct sellers and personally working with lakhs of associates for more than a decade has been condensed in this book to give you all the information you will need before you make your opinion and decision. This is an insider's view of the industry from someone who has been there, has been living it, and has attained massive success.

Please note, I don't want to convince you about starting a direct selling business. I respect you. You are unique. I don't know if this business is for you, or whether you are made for this business. Doing it or not is entirely your decision; I just want this decision to be a well-informed one.

Please also note, this book is for everyone who wants to succeed in life, and not just for direct sellers. It clearly explains the new knowledge set, skill set and mindset required to survive and thrive in the new economy. This book is a masterplan to live a good life. It's about how you can easily design the life of your dreams. Every chapter is full of soul-stirring transformative ideas that will make you question wrong beliefs and help you be aware of what is coming next and how you can prepare yourself for the same. It's your guidebook for the future.

There are chapters that will surprise and amaze you. There are tools that you can instantly apply to uplift your success and quality of life. There are solutions and breakthrough ideas to propel you faster towards your dream life. It's like the wisdom of a lifetime brought to you in an easy-to-understand and easy-to-apply format.

This is a unique, one-of-its-kind book that will give you so many different angles and perspectives of looking at the field of direct selling. Actually, there is much more to this business than just making money. Even if you don't want to make it your career, this business can help you in so many ways. Selling and contacting people is only one small part of the work that you do. You may be surprised to see that this is one of the most socially and spiritually uplifting businesses to engage in. It's strange but true—this business is like an ocean, and what people see is only a bucket of water. I want to give you the full picture in this book. What you are holding in your hands is the combined knowledge and wisdom of lakhs of people across the globe accumulated over thirteen years that will help you look at this business objectively.

Trust me, the biggest chains that confine us are not outside but within us. The biggest problem we face is not resources but our mindset. This book intends to work on our thinking and win the battle that is raging inside our head. This book is about looking at things differently. The same situation appears to be both a threat and an opportunity to different people, only because of their mindset.

Your mind is amazing. Once opened up by a new idea, your mind will never go back to its original dimension. And this book will open up some amazing possibilities for you.

The values of this business excite me so much that even after thirteen years in the business, I feel I am more driven today than ever before. I support this industry because of the values it works on and the great contribution it makes in building a better world and a better future for generations to come.

The greatest danger for most of us is not that our aim is too high and we miss it, but that it is too low and we reach it.

–Michelangelo

This book is my invitation to you to join me in this journey to explore more about you, your dreams, and all that may help you in accomplishing your dreams faster. Just embrace every word of this book with an open heart and explore it for yourself. I really want to see you happy and successful. That is my biggest reward and that's the number one reason why I do what I do.

I want you to stand up for your dreams. I want you to believe that you have everything it takes to reach great heights. I want you to start working for your dreams and surprise yourself and the world with what you can achieve.

Your partner in success,

Deepak Bajaj

DEEPAK BAJAJ'S DIRECT SELLING JOURNEY

The transformation of Deepak Bajaj from a shy village boy, born in a government employee family, to one of the top performers and leading experts in the direct selling industry is a source of inspiration and strength for everyone. Deepak has come a long way and is living proof of what can be achieved with clear vision, absolute faith, right values and commitment.

Deepak was born in a family of government employees in a small village of Haryana, India. Given the transferrable nature of the parents' jobs, the family moved towns periodically, and Deepak studied in different Hindi medium government schools. Following his B.Com degree, he cleared the CAT exam and completed his MBA from a leading management institute. Deepak had a corporate job for four years and was holding a prestigious position in a leading automobile MNC when he started a direct selling business in 2007.

Somebody approached Deepak with a direct selling business idea in 2006, but he was not convinced. Thirteen months later, he set up his now-famous ninety-day game plan, created several records, and resigned his job three months after starting the business. He was great, but his teammates couldn't duplicate his success. He didn't have any training system in place and his business came crashing to the ground, putting his family through their worst financial crisis for the next nine months. It was a tough phase and any ordinary person in his shoes would easily have quit. Instead, Deepak worked hard, applying the philosophy that whatever doesn't break you only makes you stronger.

He became a student of the business and started learning the best success practices across the globe. He then created programmes and systems that were never heard of in the industry and set record after record in the business. He faced many challenges on the way and some of his teams crashed, but with every failure, he improved his systems and created tools to support and nurture the ever-growing business.

Lakhs of people have already fulfilled their dreams and achieved top levels of expertise in their companies using his tools and systems. Deepak's book—*Be A Network Marketing Millionaire*—is one of the most read and recommended books in the entire industry. It has been translated in six languages and has been on bestseller charts ever since it was launched. It's a definitive guidebook for those looking to make a mark in this industry, one that is full of tools, techniques and strategies on every topic in direct selling.

With his thirteen incredible years of experience, Deepak has become a brand unto himself and is considered a living legend in the direct selling industry. He is a social media influencer and his videos are watched in 100+ countries. He received the Best Debut Author of the Year 2018 award and has been featured in various magazines, including making it to the cover of a magazine. He is an international NLP master practitioner and has received training from the world's best trainers in USA, Singapore, Europe, Bangkok and India. He is financially free for more than a decade now and heads an ever-expanding business empire. He loves travelling, adventure sports, marathons and reading.

His live events always run houseful because of their powerful international content, unique NLP-based methodology and real-life tools and techniques that give instant results and lasting transformation to its participants. Deepak's online network marketing course is one of the best programmes available that enables any student to scale levels within just a few sessions. He is constantly adding new online courses to help people succeed faster.

Deepak's life mission is to empower people to be the best they can be. His greatest joy comes from seeing people fulfil their dreams. He has always been working on creating tools and techniques that can help people achieve their goals faster.

Stay connected with Deepak on various social media platforms and find out more about him and his work at www.deepakbajaj.biz.

TABLE OF CONTENTS

1

Better Way to Fulfil Life's Responsibilities and Basic Needs

You cannot escape the responsibility of tomorrow by evading it today.

–Abraham Lincoln

The primary reason why most of us work is because we have responsibilities. We all need food, clothes, a house to live, and many other basics to survive. We bear responsibility for so many things—education of our children, healthcare for the entire family, maintaining status and lifestyle, social obligations and unexpected contingencies. All this needs money, and so we go to work everyday to earn this money.

Money is the key driver for people throughout their career. At the start of their career, people look for a job with the highest salary and once they take it up, they continue to look for jobs with better salaries.

Yes, there are people who will argue that money is not everything and there are other things that matter, such as the pure joy of work, job satisfaction, personal development, passion, etc. I agree that all these things are also important, but only along with our paycheck. We need money not only for today but also for tomorrow.

I believe if money is one of the key reasons for going to work, then you should choose work that satisfies these three conditions:

1. Your income is secure for years to come.
2. You get to determine how much you will earn.
3. You can increase your income whenever you want.

Responsibility finds a way. Irresponsibility makes excuses.

–Gene Bedley

If you look objectively at direct selling as a career opportunity and are committed to develop it like a serious business venture, you will realize that it's a better way to fulfil your basic needs and responsibilities. It meets all three conditions mentioned above for the kind of job or work you should choose. You are in total control of your income and no one can terminate you from your direct selling business. The irony is that people don't put in even one-tenth of their time and commitment to build this business compared with what they put in at a typical office job.

Please remember that when I say 'earn more income faster', I definitely don't want you to think of direct selling as a lottery or a get-rich-quick scheme. What I am proposing is this: If you put into direct selling those eight to twelve hours that you put in in your current job/profession, you will be able to earn more money, that too with your freedom intact.

All your talent, hard work, capability and motivation is useless, if all of it is not put on the right platform.

–Deepak Bajaj

Yes, I enjoy an incredible life today, living in a mansion with a collection of luxury cars, fame and recognition, celebrity lifestyle, having already travelled to twenty-seven countries, and so on. But when I first started the direct selling business in 2007, I simply calculated two things:

1. Whatever ten to twelve hours I am investing in my job, if I invest the same hours in this business, can I earn at least twice or thrice my salary?

2. Can I build a secure financial future for me and my family by running this business for the next five to ten years?

When my answer to both these questions was yes, I simply made the decision to start my direct selling business alongside my job. Initially, I worked on it part-time after office hours and on holidays, but once my business was established and I was confident about it, I resigned from my job and took up direct selling as a full-time career.

To be honest, when I started my business in 2007, I didn't care about passive income. Hailing from a middle-class family, I could not even believe that there is something called passive income and wondered whether it is really possible to set up a business in such a way that once established, it will continue to give me money for decades to come even without my presence.

I was an honest and committed employee in my job. Most of my colleagues switched to other companies for a 10-30 per cent raise in salary, but I continued working in the same company. When the opportunity for direct selling came my way, I had only one consideration: If I could earn double or triple my salary by working the same number of hours, why shouldn't I switch? When people don't mind switching jobs for a few extra thousands, here was a chance for me to simply double or triple my income. This one reason was enough for me to jump in and give it a shot.

I know exactly what challenges people face at different stages of this business because I have seen it all myself and in the case of lakhs of associates in my team. That is the reason why I launched our online training courses, especially to support all those people who are building this business part-time. They may not be able to attend my live workshops, but they shouldn't miss the opportunity to learn from the powerful system that empowered me to resign my job in just ninety days.

I strongly believe direct selling is a wonderful opportunity that enables you to fulfil all your basic needs properly and live a good life.

Your life is a result of the choices you have made. If you don't like your life, start making better choices.

–Zig Ziglar

2
Ticket to Lasting Happiness

Happiness is not something readymade. It comes from your own actions.

–Dalai Lama

I always believe that happiness is something internal; it doesn't really depend on outside elements. But the fact remains that a vast majority of people spend most of their waking hours at work and, hence, a person who is not happy at the workplace cannot be happy in general. If your work environment doesn't support your happiness and growth, you will always be in stress.

When it comes to work, you are the happiest when:

- ✓ You do what you love.
- ✓ You get appreciated for what you do.
- ✓ You work with dignity.

- ✓ Your work is appropriately rewarded.
- ✓ You are respected.
- ✓ You have security.
- ✓ You work with people of your choice.
- ✓ You make decisions.

You are lucky if you have all of this in your current job or profession, but for most people, all these things remain a distant dream. Many willingly compromise and adjust in their jobs with the hope that one day, they will get all these things at their workplace. Many others are stuck for years in the wrong job. They wanted to do something else, but got lured into their current job or profession because it looked financially viable and more profitable. They forgot that money comes only with excellence and excellence is really hard to achieve if you don't put your heart and soul into your work. The most frustrating thing is that, with every passing day, people get stuck deeper in the rut.

To make matters worse, most of the people I come across even complain of being underpaid at work. Despite all their compromises, they are not able to have the lifestyle they seek and that adds to the unhappiness.

I have done my MBA, worked at a corporate job for 4 years, and have been a direct selling entrepreneur for 13 years now. I have trained and coached more than 7,00,000 people in my career. With all this experience, I firmly believe that we should look at our workplace not merely as a means to earn money but as a place that will bring us great fulfilment and joy.

I found direct selling highly rewarding because not only did it give me many times more money than my job did, but it also provided me with great fulfilment and absolute joy of work every single day. I highly recommend that people explore direct selling part-time alongside whatever they are doing, so they can find out the truth for themselves. Honestly speaking, I first started direct selling solely in order to make more money, but once I realized that I was feeling happier and more fulfilled here, I chose to make it my full-time career.

Recognition and appreciation are basic human needs and these form the core values of the direct selling business. Mutual respect, recognition, teamwork, supporting one another, nurturing relationships, etc., are not optional but compulsory aspects of direct selling.

Moreover, financial security for your family is a key factor behind your happiness. I have personally experienced that scarcity of money is one of the main reasons for arguments and unhappiness in families. A direct selling business allows you to build a solid second income for your family. This added financial abundance only multiplies your happiness.

Don't build your life on momentary happiness. Build it on lasting happiness. This is done by living your passion, not your impulses.

–Unknown

I strongly believe that happiness is your birthright. Happiness should be your life compass and you should design your life in such a way that you get to do more of what gives you happiness and fulfilment every single day of your life. Let everything else come and go, but happiness and everlasting joy should become permanent for you. In all my live events, we make sure that all our workshop participants master the real-life tools and techniques required to make happiness second nature to them.

I have realized that the key to happiness lies in control. The more control you have, the happier you are. By control, I don't mean power or authority in the literal sense, but your ability to control some of the simple things in your life, such as your daily choices, daily schedules, your income, whom you meet, what you do, your working hours, and so on. The more control and freedom you have to take decisions on these aspects, the happier you will be. A large number of people have zero or very little control over any of these things. How can you ever be happy if you have given over the control of so many key aspects of your life to so many other people?

Also, happiness comes from living your life on your terms with dignity. One of the reasons why I resigned my high paying job in 2007 was to live with dignity and honour. Howsoever, good you are as a person, you will have to face all kinds of people who will say and do all kinds of nasty things to you. They may be your boss, your manager, your bankers, or anyone around you. I didn't want to be pushed into doing things that I didn't want to do. I am a nice guy who never bothered anyone, but at the same time, I wanted to create a situation for myself where I will not be bullied or cornered by anyone. I was looking for an opportunity to do that, and the moment it arrived, I latched onto it and created the life I wanted for myself.

Although happiness itself seems to be a distant dream for many, I believe there exists something beyond happiness, and interestingly, direct selling can take you there as well. That state of emotion beyond happiness is called fulfilment.

Only those who have learned the power of sincere and selfless contribution experience life's deepest joy: true fulfilment.

–Tony Robbins

The feeling of fulfilment comes from serving others and being a part of their success story. Fulfilment comes from constant growth and significant contribution in the lives of others. I want to inspire you today to aspire for fulfilment in life. Can you please answer this question for me: How many people are better off today because you lived? What if you can play a role in others' self-discovery and their journey to be the best they can be. It's a different kind of satisfaction and fulfilment to see others achieving their goals and dreams with your contribution.

Just imagine a life where you are not only taking care of your family, but you are also empowering many others to take the best possible care of their families. To me, that is a life of significance, a life well lived, and direct selling gives an opportunity to each and everyone of you to live a life of significance and everlasting fulfilment.

There was this distributor who sold his motorcycle to start a business with me, and within two years, he went on to own a premium Skoda car. One hotel management graduate from Australia started a business with me, and today, he is driving his own Audi. Trust me, to be part of people's success journey is many times more fulfilling than all the money in your bank account.

The direct selling model has been designed in such a way that you will grow only when you help others in your team to grow. Direct selling instils in you this firm belief that you just cannot grow in isolation. Many books and speakers will advise you that if you want to fulfil your dreams, just help others in fulfilling their dreams, but nobody really tells you how to do it. Direct selling is the answer. As your pursue building a successful direct selling business, you will automatically be helping many others make their dreams come true. Direct selling is a door that opens the way to ultimate happiness and lasting fulfilment.

A feeling of fulfilment is something greater than a feeling of happiness. And fulfilment doesn't come from proving someone wrong or winning a debate or getting the first rank. Fulfilment comes from doing good to others. Selflessly.

–Pratik Shelke

3

Simple Route for Anyone to Build a Second Income Source

It's true that money is not the most important thing in life, but money does affect everything that is important to life.

–Robert T Kiyosaki

In all my live events and workshops, every time I ask people to write down their goals, money and financial security is at the top of the list for most. Everyone needs financial security for themselves and for their families. Simply put, financial security is having enough money to maintain one's current lifestyle and to have sufficient bank balance to meet contingencies both today and in the future.

In 2007, when I used to invite people to join direct selling, my favourite sales pitch was: 'If you want to meet your basic needs, keep working in your job or profession, but if you want to fulfil your dreams, you should come to direct selling.' But in the current scenario, leave aside dreams; if you want to maintain a good enough lifestyle and want to ensure basic financial security for yourself, you need to have aminimum of two sources of income.

Talk to any financial adviser or wealth manager and they will tell you that having a second source of income today is not an option but a necessity. Job security is a thing of the past; competition is like never before, the speed of technical innovation is mindboggling, and business models giving excellent returns today can become redundant in no time. The old life plan that was taught to me in my school and which my father and grandfather has successfully worked on—study well, get good grades, get a good job, and continue till retirement—has crashed. It does not exist anywhere except in your head. Today, you have two choices:

1. Keep praying that nothing will go wrong with you and the government and God will take care of everything, or,
2. Start building a second income source while the first one is doing fine. The best time to prepare for retirement is not when you have retired but when you are at the peak of your career.

I am not against jobs; I was raised thanks to my mother's job. I was also an employee in the initial stages of my career. But I want you to be aware of ground realities. Changing jobs is like changing beds in a hospital, thinking that you get cured faster on a new bed. Changing jobs is a temporary solution for a permanent problem.

In this scenario, I strongly believe everyone must work on creating a good second income source. Stand up for yourself. Be smart. Control your future. Your degrees are good, but your bank will look at your profit-and-loss account and not your mark sheet. These are scary times for people who are not willing to change. But if you are willing to upgrade your skills, identify the right opportunities, and are committed to taking action, you are living in the most favourable age on earth to start anything new. The entire ecosystem is supporting people with ideas, start-ups, entrepreneurs, and even part-time freelancers.

The best way to predict the future is to create it.

–Peter Drucker

To develop a second income source, you will need any one or all of these: Knowledge, experience, mentorship, time and capital. Most people don't have any one or more of these, and hence they are not able to create a second income source for themselves.

Interestingly, the direct selling model has been created in such a way that you don't need too much time or money to build this business. You have unlimited access to people who have knowledge and experience in building this business and, more importantly, who are willing to help you in building it too. These people will help you because they will also be benefitted when you grow in this business. To top it all, every good direct selling company and team have a training and development system that will impart all the necessary skills and tools to you and your team to help you build a successful business.

Think about it. How can you ever become rich and secure without a second income source? It's mandatory. If you are an employee or professional who keenly desires becoming rich, you have to choose either of these two options:

1. Quit your job and start a full-time business, or,
2. If you are scared of that but still want to be rich, keep your job and find ways to build a second income source.

You can give me a thousand excuses as to why you can't do it, but if you have a strong desire and just one strong enough reason to actually do it, I am sure you will find a way. I understood this long back—those who don't want to do it will find an excuse, and those who really want to do it will find a way.

Direct selling is a simple, doable and time-tested way to build a second income source for anyone. It's such a boon that you can build this amazing business part-time without affecting your job or profession.

There is no one who would guarantee you the security, financial independence and the lifestyle you want, except yourself.

–Haisah Aisya Joohary

4
Real-Life Leadership

If your actions inspire others to dream more, learn more, do more and become more, you are a leader.

–John Quincy Adams

I believe leadership is not a title but a relationship. It's not any more about sitting on a chair and giving commands. It's about connection, influence, and driving results in an empowering way. You lead people not by your words, but by your presence and by the way you live your life. This definition of leadership is different from what is taught in B-Schools and what is prevalent in most places. But it is the future of leadership, and this is the type of leadership that will continue to survive and that will be expected from individuals in organizations.

Remember, leadership is not an optional but essential quality for success in any endeavour. Wherever you are, whatever you do, leadership is essential for you to rise above and make an impact. I would also like to bring to your kind attention that it's not just corporates that need leadership; leadership is required everywhere in life. Each one of us has an obligation to be a leader. That is what I mean by real-life leadership.

Everyone is a leader and leadership is to be demonstrated every single day.

–Deepak Bajaj

Right this moment, make a decision to rise and assume a leadership role wherever you are. My definition of real-life leadership is simple: Whatever you are doing, do it in such a way that there is a divine touch in your work, and you uplift fellow human beings in some way or the other. Imagine if doctors, teachers, lawyers, engineers, chartered accountants, police officers, and everyone can adopt this real-life leadership philosophy, how much we could elevate the quality of life for all of mankind.

My father-in-law, Dr S.K. Banerjee, was one such leader I have known. He was a doctor by profession and strove to be among the finest in the field. Fundamentally, people visit a doctor to cure a disease or disorder. But when people used to visit Dr Banerjee, not only did he heal their disease, but he also touched people by his conduct and inspired them to do more and be more.

He had more money than he could count, but he lived the simplest possible lifestyle. He had read several scriptures and was a follower of Swami Vivekananda. He was a philanthropist, he charged minimum fees, prescribed the lowest-priced drugs, was always calm, spoke less, had a daily morning and evening exercise routine, and followed a daily journaling and spiritual practice for years. He had a personality like the ocean, keeping unfathomable faith in God, so that no setback could shake him. His mere presence and minimum spoken words could inspire anyone in five minutes in ways that probably a high-ticket motivational seminar cannot do.

I consider this to be real-life leadership. And you must strive to develop this kind of leadership in yourself. You should develop such positive vibes that your every interaction with others will add some value in their lives. One of my dreams is to create a system that can instil this sense of leadership in everyone. I am already working on my mission with my books, videos, workshops, online courses, social media activities, and have planned a wide range to tools to expand my work and touch millions of people across the globe.

Leadership is not about titles, positions or flowcharts. It is about one life influencing another.

–John C. Maxwell

This leadership doesn't really come from classrooms and textbooks. It is purely experiential. In organizations, no one will ask you to take up a leadership role so that you can get practice or experience. Rather, you will be given a platform to lead only after you have demonstrated leadership qualities. So where do you go to learn this kind of leadership? If you explore deeply enough, I am sure you can find several places, but I know one place that can definitely transform you and put you in a role of real leadership—direct selling.

I used to lead people during my job too, but the impact and transformation that my speeches are bringing about now is beyond imagination. I am able to connect with the heart of my audience even if I am addressing 10,000 people. We laugh, we cry, we share life stories in all our events, and every session transforms people to the core. My calendar is always full months in advance. People are surprised as to how come companies are willing to pay such heavy fees for my talks. The reason is the results I deliver for them, and that comes only from the thirteen years of real-life leadership experience that direct selling has given me.

On the face of it, direct selling may appear to be a money-making machine, but what it really does is to provide an environment that truly inspires people to come out of their shells, break their limiting beliefs, go beyond their fears and go for their dreams. Only real leaders can do that, and to me, direct selling is a leader-creation factory that generates such true leaders.

Five key aspects of leadership that direct selling teaches you:

- ✓ Charisma and influence
- ✓ Team management
- ✓ Delivering results without exerting authority
- ✓ Creating followers without formal authority
- ✓ Delivery of results

So if your idea of leadership matches mine, try it. It did magic in my life; it can do the same in yours too.

A leader is one who knows the way, goes the way and shows the way.

–John C. Maxwell

5
Passive Income and Financial Freedom

A big part of financial freedom is having your heart and mind free from worry about the what–ifs of life.

–Suze Orman

I think financial freedom is a situation wherein we can maintain our current lifestyle and not worry about future contingencies, that too without having to go to work. In spite of graduating from one of the best management institutes in the country and working with a leading MNC for many years, I never knew about financial freedom and passive income until I came to direct selling.

Wealth is a measure of a person's ability to survive so many days forward.

–R. Buckminster Fuller

Being born and brought up in a family of government employees, it was drilled into me that we need to work till our retirement. This plan sounded excellent, but over a period of time, two problems have arisen—jobs are not guaranteed till one attains sixty years of age anymore and everyone's health is deteriorating. These two trends clearly indicate that whatever number of healthy and productive years we have, we must work in such a way that we have surplus money coming in every month, and at the same time, we must build a system that will continue to bring in money even when we are not able to work. This system will create financial freedom for us.

I highly recommend that to create financial freedom, choose work that can give you the following:

- More income than your expenses, resulting in surplus every month
- The power to increase your income at any time
- Possibilities of exponential growth in income
- Passive income

While we have already discussed the first three, let me explain passive income here. Passive income is automatic income wherein you create an income-producing asset or a business system in such a way that once it has been created, it will continue to give you ongoing income without your active involvement.

There are many ways to build passive income, such as investing in return-yielding real estate, building a system-driven business, dividends from stocks, royalties from the continued sales of a book, creating ground-breaking music or movies, video monetization, affiliate marketing, etc. The only challenge with all these methods is that they need huge monetary investment, knowledge or special talent and involve risk. Since on an average, people lack ability to tap into any or all of these methods, they cannot create passive income even after many years of service.

Over the decades, direct selling has proved to be a vehicle for creating passive income and financial freedom for any person, irrespective of factors such as age, education, financial position, experience, location, etc. When developed correctly, direct selling is an amazing system-driven business with unlimited possibilities.

Let me explain to you the power of this business with reference to Metcalfe's Law.

$$\text{Income (I)} = \text{Number of Active Associates (N)}^2$$

When you start a direct selling business, you are the only person in your team, and your income (I) is square of 1 (N). As you build a team of associates, your N starts increasing, and so does your income. Every distributor in a direct selling business is like a master franchiser who can appoint franchisees in his or her team. When your associates further build their teams, it adds to your team and starts increasing your N. As your N increases, your I also starts increasing.

There is immense power in the network. All the richest people in the world build networks. From Bill Gates to Jeff Bezos, Mukesh Ambani to Mark Zuckerberg, all of them have built networks. But every person cannot be Bill Gates or Mukesh Ambani. Direct selling gives you the same power that it has given to these people so that you can build your own network and enjoy exponential growth.

Everything runs on networks. How do rumours spread? How does a good movie become a hit? One person telling a few others, and they in turn telling yet others...and that's how it spreads like wild fire. Direct selling has monetized this concept. Opening your eyes is not enough; you need to open your mind. Airbnb, Uber, Facebook, YouTube, all have become top players in their respective industries simply by harnessing the power of the network.

But having people on your team is not enough; you need to develop them. There is a training and development system at work in every good direct selling team that develops these associates into active business-building distributors. As the number of active associates in your team increases, your income multiplies exponentially, gradually shaping up into a powerful passive income system.

When I started the business in 2007, I was under the illusion that everyone who started a direct selling business would acquire passive income. But as a matter of fact, only 1 per cent of direct sellers enjoy passive income, and others keep working on active income. The reason is simple—not using tools and systems. It is tools and systems that will take your business into auto mode and give you passive income.

Let me give you a real-life example. Someone from my Bangalore team called me to check how our company proposal is better than a particular other company. I could have answered his query in five minutes. Instead, I asked him to go to the 'Tools' Section of my book, *Be A Network Marketing Millionaire*, and read the chapter titled *'Universal Framework of Selecting the Best Company'*. This person called me back in five minutes after reading that chapter to say that he could now answer any questions on this matter.

Please understand thatthe best part of this story is not that he got the answer to his question, but that he found a resource where he could find all the answers he needed. So the next time he needs to call me, he will turn to this book and get the answer right there. What I have done in this case is to create an independent leader. Similarly, what we do through our workshops and online courses too, is to create independent leaders. When you have an army of independent associates, you automatically start getting passive income that keeps increasing month after month.

In [the] direct selling business, our main job is the development and nurturing of our people to empower them to build their business.

–Deepak Bajaj

Direct selling gives you financial education. This is an entirely different kind of education that is not being taught in any college or university. Only people who have already been there and achieved financial freedom can teach you the same.

Financial education fundamentally answers questions such as:

- ✓ What kind of money do you make?
- ✓ How much money do you keep?
- ✓ How can you multiply your money?
- ✓ How will you arrive at your financial freedom blueprint?
- ✓ How hard does your money work for you?
- ✓ How to build systems that continue to generate money for you without your active involvement
- ✓ How many generations can you pass on the money to?
- ✓ What are the income-generating assets you should build?

Your uplines (your seniors in the direct selling business) will mentor you and work with you for your financial freedom. When you attend my live workshops or my online course, one of the key things I do with you is to make your financial freedom blueprint.

Stocks, rental property, and other such instruments, are all good but very risky if you don't know how to handle them. SIPs (Systematic Investment Plans) and mutual funds look safe, but you don't know who is managing them and your future is always in somebody else's hands.

For so many years, my mother and I used to argue about saving for the future rather than enjoying life today. My mother used to say that we should save money for the future and I used to argue that when tomorrow is uncertain, why not enjoy with our money today. For years we could not come to a conclusion, but now I have found it and am sharing my solution to the problem here—earn so much money that you can spend to enjoy your today and at the same time save for tomorrow. Earning more is the solution.

Building our own business is the best way to become rich. After you have built your business and you have [a] strong cash flow, then you can begin investing in other assets.

–Robert T. Kiyosaki

I have another interesting question for you: Are you working for money or for wealth? Honestly speaking, a few years ago, I didn't know that these two were different. Working for money may give you instant money, but you are chained to your work and you will have to continue working for as long as you want money. The more money you want, the more you need to work. It's dangerous because if you are not able to work for some reason, instantly, the money stops coming in. As you age, this fear will grip you more and more. The worst problem in most cases is that people don't realize this till it's too late.

Working for wealth is powerful. It's a game changer. But you need a different mindset to work for wealth. Income may be small for the first few years, but it will grow exponentially when you have put the right system in place. Once you establish it with the right foundation, it will continue to bring in money even when you stop working.

I highly recommend that you should work for wealth and not for money. There are countless ways to do that. Find out what works for you. If you don't know how to begin, then start building a direct selling business. Just make sure you work with the right company and, more importantly, work with the right mentor and build business with the right foundation. I can't wait to see you financially free.

Your financial statement is your report card after you leave school.

–Robert T. Kiyosaki

6
Total Personality Makeover

When you achieve a goal, the important thing is not what you get, but what you become in the process of achievement of that goal.

–Deepak Bajaj

There is a hidden benefit in direct selling—it changes you completely and makes you a better person. I have realized that everyone loves to talk about change, but no one really wants to change. Among those who genuinely want to change, many of them are trying but are not able to make it happen. Actually, people change when change is the only option available to them. It's so funny that sometimes, during my live talks, when I ask people whether I can give them an experience of change, they immediately say—'No, please give us a talk on change.' People are more interested in talk about change than actually going through change!

We all understand that age-old maxim—'If you keep doing whatever you have been doing, you will keep getting whatever you have been getting.' But most people stay stuck and keep doing the same things they started doing many years ago. Same work, same routine, same people to deal with. In fact, a vast number of people never undertake any new educational course or training after they graduate from college or university.

Your life does not get better by chance; it gets better by change.

–Jim Rohn

Direct selling is a powerful dream-fulfilling business that not only inspires you to change but also forces you to make all the necessary changes in your life. Firstly, you see so many rewards by embracing the changes that you commit yourself to change. In fact, the entire process—from joining a direct selling company to becoming successful—has been designed in such a way that it requires you to constantly change and improve.

Every good direct selling team has a powerful training and support system that gives regular training sessions to improve various aspects of your personality. Some of the key changes that building a direct selling business brings about in you are:

- ✓ Ever-smiling nature
- ✓ Optimism
- ✓ Respecting others
- ✓ Patience
- ✓ Time management
- ✓ Personal hygiene
- ✓ Better dressing style and choice of clothes
- ✓ Manners and etiquettes
- ✓ Improved dealings with people
- ✓ Self-confidence
- ✓ Your choice of words

So if you are looking for a total personality makeover, direct selling is the right choice for you. Don't do this business for anything else but to totally transform your personality, and if you love the values of this business, take it up seriously. Earn money, be a better person, and fulfil all your dreams.

Every next level of success will demand a new version of you.

–Deepak Bajaj

Other than the above-mentioned changes, there is one particular part of personality that remains underdeveloped in many cases. This is a mandatory skill for growth and success in every field of life; it is called emotional intelligence. Even though this skill is vital, our parents, schools, colleges, and the entire education system has totally ignored the development of this skill.

If you cannot control your emotions, you cannot control your money.

–Warren Buffet

The direct selling field is a good training ground to develop your emotional intelligence. Your commitment, patience and perseverance will be tested here every single day. Your core values, including optimism, hope, faith and gratitude, will be put to test every single day. You will have to learn to handle anger, frustration, rejection, ridicule, disappointments, etc. This is the only way you develop emotional intelligence and this is the kind of education that you need to get to the top.

Let me share an incident from the life of Thomas Elva Edison. Not only was he the inventor of the light bulb, he was also the founder one of the most successful companies in the world—General Electric. One of the core reasons behind his great success was not his scientific knowledge alone, but his emotional intelligence and perseverance. He failed repeatedly in so many projects and ventures, yet his emotional resilience made him continue to pursue his dreams. Once, there was a catastrophe when his laboratory and factory caught fire. While the factory was burning to ashes, he asked his son to quickly call his mother, saying, 'Quickly call your mother. She won't get a chance to see this kind of a fire again.' In today's valuation, his loss was a few hundred crores, but standing on the remains on his factory, he said, 'Now all my mistakes have burnt with this fire. I have a golden opportunity to start afresh now.' Within the next few years, he rebuilt a much better factory and laboratory. This is what we all need to learn from Edison and apply in our lives.

Direct selling will provide you with ample opportunities to grow every single moment, because you are dealing with people all the time.

You will deal with people who are ambitious and people who are lazy and procrastinate, those who quit, those who lie, those who will demand more of you and those who will throw you out of your comfort zone. Direct selling will test your EI (Emotional Intelligence) many times every day and improve it with every interaction. If you meet Gaurav Bajaj today and you knew what he was like when he started this business with me in 2007, you will be shocked at his personality makeover. He used to sweat and shiver while talking to two people, and today he is among the top direct sellers in the country.

Enhanced EI will enhance the total quality of your life and will give you a complete personality makeover. You will find it easier to talk to people, communicate much better, and handle your emotions more effectively. You will be a better investor, better manager and an excellent leader. You will negotiate better, handle teams more effectively, your marriage will improve, you will be a better parent, and you will have better relationships.

Every success story is a tale of constant adaptation, revision and change.

–Richard Branson

7
Develop a New Empowering Mental Blueprint

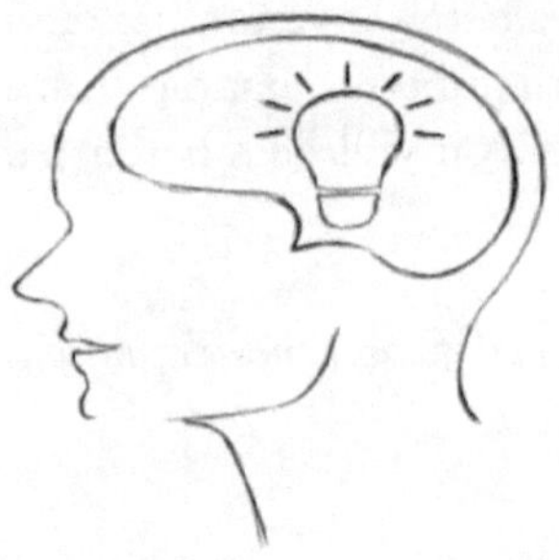

Visualize this thing you want. See it, feel it, believe in it. Make your mental blueprint and begin.

–Robert Collier

Everything we do and achieve is a reflection of everything that is inside us. All our actions, accomplishments, behaviours, and how we handle people and situations is a reflection of our mental blueprint. Our mental blueprint is our map of the world, composed of our beliefs and values. It's simply how we look at ourselves and the world around us. It determines everything in our life, including our success, health, happiness, relationships and self-esteem.

In terms of cause and effect—our mental blueprint is the cause and our achievements and behaviour are the effect. Each one of us has a unique blueprint, one that has developed over the years. Everything we have faced in life, our experiences with people and situations, our family, our upbringing and all our encounters with life have a bearing on this blueprint which we carry with us wherever we go. It serves as a guidebook that helps us operate our life, shaping all our decisions and actions. It is immensely powerful and governs and determines the quality of our life.

Interestingly, for most people, all the engraving of events and experiences on this blueprint happens unconsciously, with layer after layer getting accumulated and moulding it into a whole. Why is it that people struggle to change their life even though they consciously do want to change? Why do some people get excited when a new opportunity presents itself, whereas others just shut themselves off from it? The answer to both lies in the difference in their deep-rooted mental blueprint. The kind of questions people will ask you after you share your business opportunity with them is also a reflection of their distinct blueprint. It's amazing to see how this individual map dictates just about every aspect of life, even governing our reactions to different situations.

So if you want a different life, then you need a different blueprint for your life. Change your mental blueprint, and everything in your life will change as well.

Be not afraid of growing slowly; be afraid only of standing still.

–Chinese Proverb

I was born in a small village in a government employee family. The previous two generations in my family were also government employees, and we were raised with the typical middle-class values of saving money, cutting expenses, living within the budget, and so on. We bargained to get stuff for less and we shopped during sale season. It was as if asking for a concession was inherent in our very DNA. We exercised our right to get discounts everywhere—with vegetable vendors and grocers, auto rickshaws and taxis, clothes and accessories. We were appreciated when we saved even ten to twenty rupees.

Whatever you focus on grows. As a family, we were focusing on cutting expenses and saving money all the time. Just think about it—when do you operate this way? When you don't have enough money and you are certain that this situation is not going to change in the near future. This behaviour indicates that you are operating onthe presupposition of a scarcity of money. Tomorrow can be even worse, so not only must you cut expenses today, but also save for tomorrow. What will this sort of thinking produce for you as per the law of attraction? Even more scarcity in your life.

The worst thing about living this kind of life is not the compromises or poor quality of life that results from it, but the fact that you don't even realize this kind of thinking is limiting you, preventing you from growing and achieving big things in life given this approach, attitude and belief system. Moreover, since all your relatives, friends and neighbours talk and behave like this, you accept it as the right way of living. Every single day, you get used to it and some years down the line, it becomes such an intrinsic part of you that you stop questioning it altogether. Instead, you start questioning others who question this outlook on life!

Nobody ever talked about dreams in our family. How can you even talk about dreams when you have calculated the exact amount you will get as salary or pension for the rest of your life! It seemed as if dreams were a privilege not within the reach of a government employee. Corporate jobs were meant for those unfortunate few who could not get a government job. To add to this, the discussion among some of our neighbours was not about how we could add more value to our job but about how we could minimize our work.

It was not about the quality of work, but about staying in office from 9 to 5. Whatever may be the quality of work you produce, your salary and increments are fixed for the rest of your working life. When you know your income cannot grow beyond this, you plan your life accordingly. Game over.

This was the mental blueprint I inherited and nourished. My corporate job changed it slightly, but it was direct selling that totally turned it around. In the language of my mentor, Dr John Grinder, direct selling transformed my world by entirely changing my map of the world. It completely changed the way I looked at myself, my potential, and the people and the situations around me. It made me who I am today.

Some people die at 25 and aren't buried until 75.

–Benjamin Franklin

On the outside, it may appear that direct selling gave me a grand villa, a collection of luxury cars, a luxurious lifestyle, holidays to twenty-seven countries, investments, fame and recognition, and whatnot. For me, though, the biggest thing that direct selling gave me is a new winning and empowering blueprint. It changed my approach from 'I can't afford it' to 'How can I afford it'? Look at the contrast in these two statements. One is sad and limiting, while the other is empowering and inspiring. But these are not simply two random statements; this is the way of life, this is life itself. It's liberating and it opens you to possibilities you never thought existed. A change in your mental blueprint is like a rebirth and gifts you a new world of possibilities and opportunities.

Some of the core values of my new mental blueprint are:

- ✓ I can dream anything and everything.
- ✓ Once one goal is accomplished, set another one.
- ✓ I deserve the best of everything for my family and me.
- ✓ I am enough and I am ready for anything that I aspire to achieve.
- ✓ The universe is on my side and always helps me in every possible way.
- ✓ Training and growth never stops.
- ✓ My work is my opportunity to multiply my contribution and the value I add to others.
- ✓ Mistakes are welcome. Mistakes are my trophies.
- ✓ The size of my achievements is directly proportional to the number of failures I have encountered.
- ✓ Whatever doesn't break me, makes me stronger.
- ✓ It's not the situations; it's my reaction to situations that determines the quality of my life.
- ✓ Life is happening for me, and not to me.
- ✓ Patience, persistence and consistency are the golden virtues of life.

This new mental blueprint offered to me by direct selling is making me do the impossible and surprise myself and the world with what I can achieve. Everyday of my life I am living a life that is consistent with this renewed blueprint and it's propelling me to be the best I can be. In all my workshops and online courses, I always work on changing the mental blueprint of my students.

Actually, there are two voices inside us—one that encourages us to dream big and another that demands us to quit and stay wherever we are. Both these voices are really powerful, and a majority who come from a poor or middle-class background have been trained since childhood to listen to this second, defeating voice within. Direct selling brings out the dreamer in you. Your uplines and the entire system support you in dreaming bigger and constantly stretching yourself to work for your dreams. It's a beautiful mind shift that has the power to totally transform every aspect of your life.

Make your life a masterpiece; imagine no limitations on what you can be, have or do.

–Brian Tracy

Why is it essential to have dreams or work with goals? It's simply because every dream will demand you to grow, and to me, growth is the only evidence that you are alive. Fulfilling any dream is a journey; it's a process of transformation. By the time you achieve a dream, you have already grown to be a different person. When you accomplish a dream, what is important is not what you get but what you become in the process of achieving that dream.

That's the reason why I recommend that every time you accomplish a goal, it's important to set a new one immediately. Mahatria Ra says: 'The question is not from where to here, but the question actually is from here, where?' When you set out towards a goal, you had a certain mindset and capability, but now with renewed vision, a new thought process and new capabilities, just imagine all that is possible and all that can you attain....

It's never about owning a big house or a big car. It is about developing yourself in the process of getting there. Developing a new blueprint that includes working hard, making new plans, handling setbacks, learning new things, challenging the status quo, breaking mental barriers, facing rejection and ridicule, and doing what people say you cannot do. Imagine doing all of it with a smile on your face and joy in your heart. For some, it's a punishment and for some others, it's the biggest adventure of life—and that is what is dictated by their different mental blueprints.

A dream introduces you to you. When I was in Europe for my advanced international coaching certification, John Grinder told us that human beings are like onions. There are so many layers. The tragedy is that most people die without even seeing what was possible. Without ever realizing how much they could have done with their lives. When you work for a dream and surround yourself with people who are high dreamers, you stretch the boundaries of your own thinking, and your mind, once stretched, never goes back to its original dimensions. When you work sincerely to fulfil those dreams, you do more and be more, and to me, that is the true and real purpose of life.

The size of my current house is 10 times that of the house where I grew up. I don't fully use even 2 floors in my house. I have more luxury cars than members in our family. I have already travelled to 27 countries. I have more ongoing passive income that my family can spend. My business empire is expanding by the day and I believe I have just started. I have trained and coached more than 7,00,000 people at the time of writing this book in 2019. My 11 month-old YouTube channel is one of the fastest growing channels and is viewed everyday in more than 100 countries. Since its launch, my first book, *Be A Network Marketing Millionaire*, has been on bestseller charts and has been used as an essential guidebook by every direct selling company. Within one year of release, the book is already available in 6 languages and is transforming thousands of people everyday. At the end of the day, I consider my biggest reward is the impact and transformation I have been able to create in thousands of people with my work.

But when I look at all this, I firmly believe it is not even 1 percent of what I will achieve in the next five years. My team and I are passionately working on multiplying our impact and effecting transformation for millions of people across the globe. Trust me, the objective of the game is not to have all this, but to examine what I have become in the process of achieving all this. The game is the size of my new dreams and my absolute faith that I can achieve anything and everything. I understand that what got me here will not take me there, and I am super excited to see who I willnext become in the process of achieving these new goals.

In my #1 bestselling book on the subject—*Be A Network Marketing Millionaire*—which is the most widely read and recommended book among all direct selling teams, I have written a chapter on breakthrough goals. You must read that. A breakthrough goal is such a big goal that you will have to become an entirely new person to accomplish that goal. Hope you can see the depth in the point I am making here—it's not about the goal; it's about you, your growth and your mental blueprint. I always say this during my live training events—the real job is in surprising yourself with what you can do.

Continuous improvement is better than delayed perfection.

–Mark Twain

Let me summarize the process of changing your mental blueprint through the Cycle of Continuous Growth. The game is simple—set a goal. Work for it, achieve the goal, learn from the process, then set a new goal and repeat the cycle.

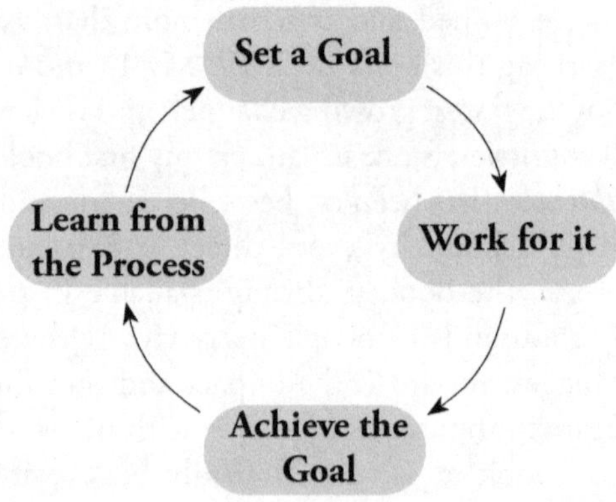

Cycle of Continuous Growth

If not for direct selling, I would have never questioned my old mental blueprint and would not have become the person I now am. And more importantly, the person I am going to become.

Don't wish it was easier, wish you were better.
Don't wish for less problems, wish for more skills.
Don't wish for less challenges, wish for more wisdom.

–Jim Rohn

8

Shortcut to Your Dreams

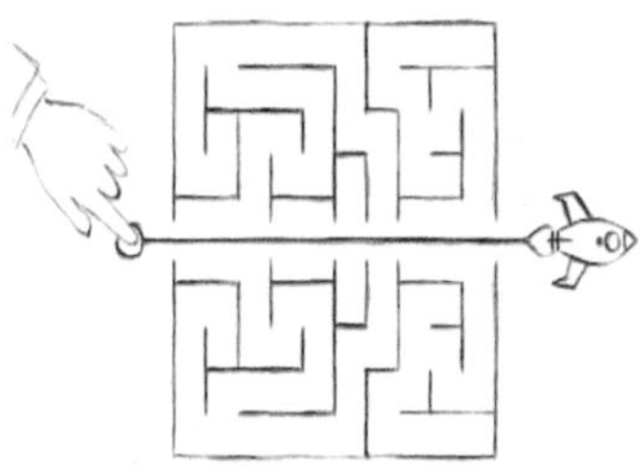

Without dreams and goals there is no living, only merely existing, and that is not why we are here.

–Mark Twain

What is a dream? Simply put, a dream is a heartfelt desire to grow and to live a better life. Among all living creatures, human beings are the only ones endowed with this great power to dream. Human beings have the capability and wisdom to utilize resources to change their situation and achieve whatever they want. This desire and capability to grow and to make things better for ourselves and for the world is God's gift to us. It's a privilege we must utilize.

This life is God's gift to us and what we achieve in this life is our gift back to God.

–Deepak Bajaj

Everyone grows up within numerable dreams in school and college years. They believe they can have anything they set their eyes on. Everyone wants to live life on their own terms. But as they move into their professional fields, they slowly leave their dreams behind and start accepting their situation almost helplessly. To me, this is the biggest tragedy, the biggest insult to God. Whatever may happen to you and irrespective of your current situation in life, you must commit to yourself that you will never, ever, give upon your dreams. Negotiate and compromise on anything in life, but never compromise on your dreams. Always remember—God never gives you a dream without the capability to make that dream a reality.

The best gift direct selling gave me is the power to dream again. I have read this quote by Napoleon Hill many times—'Whatever the mind of a man can conceive and believe, it can achieve'—but I never really believed it. Direct selling transformed my life by reinstating in me this unprecedented faith and conviction that I can dream of anything and achieve everything I want.

Dreams remain unfulfilled for most people because they don't have enough money. You need a surplus amount of money to fulfil your dreams. Surplus is the amount of money that is available to you after meeting all your basic expenses and setting aside some savings for the future.

Surplus = Income – Expenses – Savings for contingencies

For most people, there is zero surplus money available. The worst part of it is that they have never had a surplus for so many years, and the way they continue to toil, they will never have a surplus in the future either. Many people keep working under the false illusion that once they receive the next increment in their salary or professional income, they will achieve some surplus and fulfil their dreams. But the fact remains that the average employee gets only 4-7 per cent annual increment, and all of it is eaten up by inflation and in maintaining lifestyle given the general rise in cost of living. Since there is no surplus money available, people stay stuck in the same lifestyle for years on end. Some get lured into heavy personal loans towards upgrading their lifestyles and end up in a financial mess.

You just cannot fulfil your dreams if you don't have control over your income.

–Deepak Bajaj

The direct selling business gives you total control over your income.

It's your business and you decide your income and increments. In your job, your boss or the HR department will decide how much salary you will draw, but in direct selling, it is you who will decide how much you are worth. You definitely need to work hard to obtain your desired income, but I admire the fact that you have the ultimate power to set your income goals and action plans.

This power to give myself an increment whenever I wanted was a big motivation for me when I first began my direct selling business. I started off with a company that offered a weekly income. I was so excited and used to voice aloud in every meeting—'Why wait for fifty-two weeks to get an increment when you have the power to give yourself an increment every week?'

A job gives you an assurance and guarantee, but a business offers you possibilities and opportunities. A direct selling business is built on unlimited income possibilities because it's a team-based business that grows exponentially. It's a great opportunity for anyone to build a big business empire irrespective of their education level, financial background, gender, age, location, and other such factors.

I can propose a simple, doable and proven solution if you want to achieve your dream lifestyle. This worked for me and for thousands of other people whom I have trained and coached for more than a decade now.

Keep working at your day job/profession and develop your direct selling or any other part-time business in the evening hours or over weekends. When your business starts generating money, invest that money in income-generating assets. This step is critical and doable because, after all, you are already managing your expenses with your current income, so your business income is extra money that you are earning.

Gradually, you will have three incomes sources—one job, one part-time business, and an investment asset that brings in money. Keep your job and keep strengthening your business because you have unlimited wealth generation opportunity there. Keep investing the money to build more income-generating assets. That's the way to become rich and fulfil your dreams.

MASTERPLAN TO ACHIEVE YOUR DREAM LIFESTYLE

Phase	Actions & Strategies
1	Job/Profession + Build a part-time business
2	Job/Profession + Strengthen your business + Build your savings from business income
3	Job/Profession + Strengthen your business + Invest your savings in an income-generating asset
4	Job/Profession + Continue strengthening your business + Create multiple income-generating assets
5	Job/Profession is optional + Business in auto mode + keep multiplying income-generating assets and live your dream lifestyle

This is a simple plan that anyone can follow and live their dream lifestyle. The biggest problem with most of the middle class and poor strata in society is that they work throughout their whole life for only one source of income, that too one that demands their active, daily involvement at work. For all these people, direct selling is a proven and practical second source of income that has been helping people live their dreams for more than half a century now.

Let me discuss one more hidden but unbelievably powerful benefit of direct selling in fulfilling dreams. Do you know anyone who has dreams and who is willing to work, but who is still not able to make any significant progress in life? Actually, dream fulfilment requires a combination of factors as given in the diagram below:

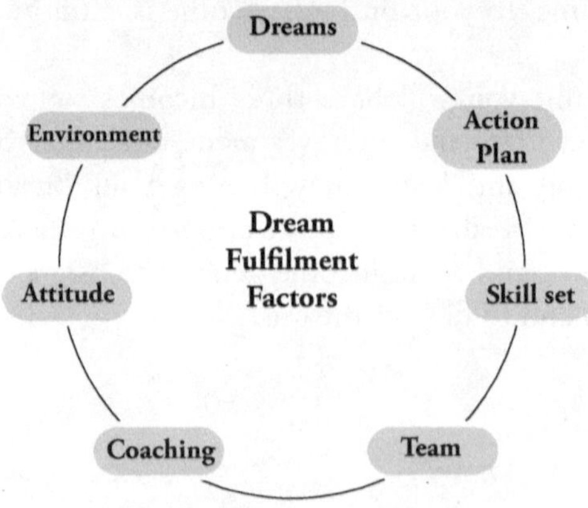

By its very design, direct selling gives you all of this combined. The direct selling business culture is such that it encourages you to chase your dreams. Your uplines will keep raising their standards higher in terms of their goal fulfilment, and you will meet so many people achieving their dreams in every meeting you attend. This will, in turn, automatically stretch and expand the size of your dreams. You will have a conducive environment, ongoing training and the right mentoring to empower you to build your team and fulfil your dreams.

How to develop these seven factors is exactly what we teach you when you take up one of my online training courses or attend my world-famous live workshops.

I believe and I have personally experienced for over a decade now that the direct selling lifestyle is one of the best on the earth. So whatever your dreams—cars, mansions, holidays, luxuries of life, financial freedom, early retirement, contributing to society, having an impact on the world—direct selling is a powerful vehicle to empower you to make them come true.

Anyone can pursue this business of endless possibilities and do it part-time at that. That's why I call this business a shortcut to your dream lifestyle. But when I say 'shortcut', please don't be under the illusion that it is going to be easy. Of course, it will be demanding, but I believe the chances of fulfilling dreams through direct selling are much higher and quicker than in a typical job or profession.

Make a list of your dreams today. Make an action plan right now and quickly start taking action. You deserve it. Don't wait for miracles. Be a miracle. So many people are living their dreams—why not you? Why not now?

All our dreams can come true, if we have the courage to pursue them.

–Walt Disney

9
Right Parenting and Legacy Creation

The question isn't [so] much, are you parenting the right way? It is, are you the adult you want your child to grow up to be?

–Brene Brown

Parenting is a role that is close to every human being's heart. We all love our parents as much as we love our kids. These are bonds of a lifetime.

Each one of us wants to be a good parent and do everything possible to empower our children to be the best they can be. I have seen this with my parents, and I am sure each one of us has memories when our parents went out of their way and did all they could for us.

Parents always try to do for their children much more than what they do for themselves. They stretch themselves to do what they could never do for themselves. Direct selling is a business infused with so much humanity that this book would be incomplete if we did not discuss this most amazing bond shared by parents and children.

It's not what you do for your children, but what you have taught them to do for themselves that will make them successful human beings.

–Ann Landers

Being a child to my parents and being a parent to five children in our home, I have learnt a few things about parenting that I would like to discuss here.

I highly recommend one thing—never try to teach anything to your children. That's the job of the school. Don't try to be their teacher; they hate most of their teachers anyway. You only assume the role of a parent and not the teacher; let your home be their home, not another school. Children learn much more unconsciously than what they learn consciously. Most of their learning happens by observing people and situations and then processing this observation through mirror neurons. This process is called unconscious assimilation.

Ever since I realized the intricacies and applications of this concept during one of my training sessions in Europe, I have been fascinated with this amazing form of learning. I am constantly researching and creating tools that can multiply learning through unconscious assimilation. Most of the work that happens in my live workshops is through games and activities that unconsciously instil desired behaviours and attitudes in my participants. We bring about mental and emotional changes in you without you being aware of it. What brings magical results in my online programmes is this secret, hidden emotional and mental transformation system that is installed in every video and audio tool.

All of us have learnt so many critical things in life only through unconscious assimilation. Just think about it—which school or college taught us our speech, the choice of words we use, the way we stand or walk, our response to different people and situations, almost all of our behaviour patterns, our fears, our attitude, our risk-taking capacity, and so on and so forth. Just consider the fact that thousands of processes and muscle movements work together to create something as simple as the act of standing.

If we didn't get all this from schools, colleges or any formal teachers, then how did we learn all of these? Where did our unique behaviours come from? The answer is unconscious assimilation. Another amazing thing about this process is that anything learnt through unconscious assimilation stays with us for the long term, often for the rest of our lives. Many of us are living with certain attitudes and behaviours that we learnt even without our conscious knowledge, and yet we struggle for decades to change them.

Once you understand this, you will appreciate and understand what I am going to give you in the next few paragraphs as my key philosophy of parenting and life.

The voice of parents is the voice of gods, for to their children they are heaven's lieutenants.

–William Shakespeare

Your job as parents is primarily to become the human being that you want your children to be. It's really that simple. Whatever values, attitude or behaviours you want to see in your children, simply start demonstrating those yourself. Please remember, your kids will not do what you tell them to do—they will do what you do. To that extent, your sole responsibility is to grow and make yourself better. You just need to be a role model for your kids.

Now the question arises: When parents know that they need to be the right role models for their children, why do they still keep lecturing and shouting at the latter? At the same time, they complain that their kids don't listen. The logic is simple. Shouting and instructing others is much easier than improving oneself. Believe it or not, the day you honestly start working on improving yourself and getting better, you will stop shouting and preaching to your children. And what's more amazing, your children will start listening and understanding you better from that day on. Trust me and try this for the next few days, and you will feel the difference.

Once you understand this concept, you will be able to appreciate how the direct selling model of business can help you in becoming better parents.

1. The most critical resource for direct selling is—you. All training sessions and activities in direct selling are designed with one purpose alone—to constantly improve you in all different aspects of life and to make you a better human being. I personally know thousands of people who have been transformed by coming into the fold of direct selling. I myself am one of them. When your kids see you demonstrating good virtues and constantly improving yourself, they will

automatically learn all the right things, and this is the first thing you need to be a better parent.

2. One of the best things about direct selling is the life-changing education it offers. The life and soul of direct selling lies in its training events. When your kids attend these events, it will be very empowering for them and teach them the virtues of winning and right conduct right from a young age. Imagine your kids attending training on leadership, communication skills, public speaking, sales, relationships, entrepreneurship, people management, and all this from people who have already done it and mastered it. These are things you wish you had learnt when you were a kid. Now your kids can learn it all at the right age. At these events, they will meet so many real-life achievers who have transformed themselves, and regular interaction with these experts will build their faith, optimism, self-confidence, dreams and spirit.

Since you have come this far in this book, I am sure you will be an excellent parent and will raise incredible children who will make this world a better place.

Legacy is not leaving something for people. It's leaving something in people.

–Peter Strople

If you can do more, be more and be an example of personal transformation. I do think that will be the best legacy you can leave for your children and for the world. Be on a mission of constant self-improvement. Be so obsessed about bettering yourself that once in a while, when you look at yourself and your achievements, you are able to surprise yourself with how far you have come.

Why should people around you look for a hero? Why don't you be the hero for them? Yes, it takes more work to be a hero than to talk about heroes and ask others to be heroes. Why don't you adopt the philosophy of daily improvement and live those very values that you preach to people?

If you really want to create a legacy that you will be proud of, I dare you to take my 3 Step PLC test—the Primary Legacy Creator test. Please answer these three simple questions to take this test:

1. What are the three words that should come to people's minds when they think of you?
2. Be absolutely truthful and look at yourself from a third person's perspective. Now think of three words that any person would think of when they look at you as you are right now.
3. If the words you come up with for Question No. 2 are not the same as those in the answer to Question No. 1, please make an action plan for your life right now so that over a period of time, you build your life in such a way that every time people think of you, what they come up with is exactly what you have yourself mentioned in answer to Question No. 1.

You can do this in your diary, or you can take this test on the next page in the space provided there.

Of course, a direct selling business is a nomination-based business, and whatever business you develop will automatically be transferred to your children as a legacy, but be aware that all the people whose lives you touched while building this business will always remember you for your contribution in their lives. Your personal transformation will inspire people to be the best version of themselves and you will stay forever in the hearts of so many people. That's what I call a true legacy.

There are two things we should give our children: One is roots and the other is wings.

–Author unknown

Primary Legacy Creator (PLC) Test

1. What are the three words that should come to people's mind when they think of you?
    1. ______________________________
    2. ______________________________
    3. ______________________________
2. Be absolutely truthful and look at yourself from a third person's perspective. Now answer: What are the three words any person would think of when they look at you as you are right now?

1. ______________________
2. ______________________
3. ______________________

3. If your answers to Question No. 2 are not the same as those you mentioned in answer to Question No. 1, please make an action plan for your life right now so that over a period of time, you build your life in such a way that every time people think of you, what they come up with is exactly what you have mentioned in answer to Question No. 1.

____
____
____
____
____
____
____
____
____
____
____

Additionally, if you want to take this process further, you can refer to my powerful and empowering goal-setting process, called PDA, in my bestselling book, *Be a Network Marketing Millionaire*. The PDA process will not only give you the next level of clarity and conviction required to meet your goals but will also will multiply your chances of goal accomplishment.

10

Mastery of Two Essential Life Skills—Communication and Selling

Communication—the human connection—is the key to personal and career success.

–Paul J. Meyer

Communication is at the very heart of being a human being. I call it a surviving and thriving skill. You need good communication skills to survive as well as to grow in life. You may not realize it, but right from birth to death, this is the one thing each one of us is doing all the time—communicating. Every human emotion is a form of communication. Even prayer is a form of communication. Expressing yourselves through any medium is communication, and talking is just one of them. During the course of my career, I learned that some of the best forms of communication are the ones that are done without talking.

Every time you communicate, you have an intention or agenda. Sometimes, it may be explicit, while at other times, it may be hidden. But you definitely want the other person to do something as a result of your communication. The other person may be your child, spouse, friends, colleagues, audience, or just about anybody with whom you are communicating.

You may feel that communication is complete once you have expressed your point, but I believe communication is not complete till the time the other person has understood and responded to it. Communication is said to be effective only if you are able to achieve a result or get an affirmative response. You need to develop your communication skills in order to achieve this. Although good communication skills are an essential life tool, this aspect of development is often ignored at school and college levels. The faster you understand its importance and start developing it, the more rapidly you can grow in career and life. Right from a job interview to bagging promotions to dealing with colleagues, vendors, seniors, teammates, customers and suppliers, every activity needs excellent communication skills. What's the point of being good if you cannot tell the world about your goodness?

Please remember—what you have at birth is the ability to communicate but mastery in communication skills takes time and effort, and I think it's a skill that you nurture throughout life. Improving your communication skills is so critical for success that I conduct a special workshop and course only on communication skills.

Communication is a skill that you can learn. It's like riding a bicycle or typing. If you are willing to work at it, you can rapidly improve the quality of every part of your life.

–Brian Tracy

The best way to improve your communication skills is to put yourself in an environment where you communicate with a variety of people on a regular basis. Direct selling is an excellent platform for the same. People are your only resource in direct selling, and you are interacting with people all the time. In fact, some of you might not have started direct selling giving this very excuse—that it requires dealing with people!

I strongly believe in this life mantra: Every time you are offered a good opportunity and you refuse it on this basis of some excuse, please be aware that whatever your excuse is for not doing it, you can convert the same excuse into your reason for doing it. If this mandatory requirement of dealing with people has been your excuse for not doing direct selling, please flip it over and say: My reason for starting direct selling is that I want to develop my communication skills.

Direct selling not only gives you an opportunity to communicate with so many different people everyday, but it also gives you the chance to instantly evaluate the results of your communication. There are regular training programmes for the same, and you have seniors who constantly guide you and give you feedback on your improvement. As your communication skills improve, so will your success in direct selling. Improvement in communication skills will not only multiply your income in direct selling, but will also better your performance at work and raise the quality of your relationships.

Learn to sell. In business, you are always selling: to your prospects, investors and employees. To be the best sales person, put yourself in the shoes of the person to whom you are selling. Don't sell your product. Solve their problems.

–Mark Cuban

Selling is also a form of communication where the agenda is to specifically sell some product, service or idea. Selling is another essential life skill required for surviving and thriving. Selling is the lifeline of every business. Every other department spends money, but sales is the only department that brings money into the organization. What's the point in making the world's best products or services if we cannot get people to pay for it? Every single day of your life, you need to persuade, negotiate and influence people—this is also selling.

I have seen some excellent people being turned down for promotions and increments in their jobs, just because they are not good at selling. One of the key reasons why many start-ups close down is that their founders cannot generate enough sales. Sales is essential. If you cannot sell, you simply cannot become a successful businessperson or grow to the top of any career you choose to pursue.

All the best leaders are essentially the best salespeople. Mahatma Gandhi, Mark Zuckerberg, Swami Vivekananda, Narendra Modi, Dhirubhai Ambani...all these stalwarts are salespeople at heart. They have honed their selling skills to such a high scale that they can move thousands and millions of people to act. When they speak, people are inspired. It is because they have developed the power to speak directly to the spirit of the people.

Let's understand it the other way round. Just think of people who are not successful in life—who are they? They are the ones whom nobody listens to. They are the people who cannot sell. They are afraid of selling and they have associated negative mental images with the concept of selling. That's why they are stuck in the same place in their lives.

Selling is our No. 1 job. Never get away from selling a lot of merchandise personally. The more you sell, the more you learn.

–James Cash Penney

For most people, direct selling is the one assured ray of light to get rid of this fear of selling. Selling is not science or mathematics that you can learn in classrooms from textbooks. It is a street skill. It comes with the right amount of practice when you regularly go out to sell. The direct selling industry provides a supportive learning environment that enables and empowers anyone to gradually master the principles of selling.

In a typical sales job, you are terminated from the job when you don't sell, but in direct selling, you get more training and handholding from your seniors when you don't sell. They will come with you for sales calls, and will give you both on-the-job and classroom training. They will also give you emotional support and inspiration to keep going. The direct selling ecosystem makes it easier for even a non-sales person to become proficient at selling.

Many people know that direct selling involves meeting people, selling and facing rejections. It is this fear that holds them back from starting a direct selling business, even though they may give many other reasons for it. Deep down in their heart, they know that the problem is not direct selling as such; the problem is their own fearful mindset. Often, these are poor or middle-class people who are stuck in a rut all their lives. You may meet them after a gap of five years, but you will still find them at the same place where you met them five years ago. Their fear, their unwilling attitude and refusal to learn selling skills keep them confined in a life of compromise and mediocrity.

A direct selling business is an excellent training ground for sales. You get a conducive environment and a compassionate support system to learn how to sell, how to overcome your fear of rejection, how to handle your setbacks, and how to convey your point to other individuals or groups.

Learning to sell brings out the winner in you. The most successful people in the world are the most rejected people in the world. India is the world's largest democracy with over 130 crore people. The most important position in this country, the position of the prime minister, technically goes to someone who is rejected by 49 per cent of the people. This means that you can become the prime minister only if you can handle the rejection of crores of people. The bigger the rejection, the greater will be the size of your achievement!

Welcome rejections. Please remember that success begins with rejection. Whenever life throws you a challenge, don't say—why me? Instead say—try me.

Remember this classic success formula:

Rejection and Improvement = Growth and Achievement

The road to success is simple. With every rejection, ask yourself what you did wrong, and then make the necessary changes. Every rejection followed by improvement will give you growth and achievement. Bigger the size of the rejections you can handle, greater will be the scale of your achievements.

Rejection is the starting point of all achievement. The more you are rejected, the higher will be your chances of being accepted at the next meeting. Moral of the story: If you want to be successful, go out and get rejected. Seek more rejections. Be on a mission to get rejections. Get rejected more, and faster. Direct selling provides this priceless opportunity to any common person to face rejections in a supportive and compassionate environment. Spend three to five years of life doing this, and you will create an inspiring life with massive success and financial abundance.

Success is the ability to go from failure to failure without losing your enthusiasm.

–Winston Churchill

In my first week in direct selling, I got 148 rejections. But I got 25 acceptances too. The result was an income of ₹ 51,000. It was great income for a week, back in 2007 when I started. But behind this earning of ₹ 51,000 was 148 rejections that I endured. This went on for 4 weeks. I got more than 500 rejections and NOs in my first month, but this gave me an income of ₹ 2,00,000 in the first month itself. Why so many people never make the effort to earn this income is because they can't handle and accept such a large number of NOs.

This journey of dreaming, working on new things, failing, improving, and then dreaming something bigger all over again has become part of my life now. I start new things. I start new businesses. I explore new locations and just go out there and get rejected. Every rejection multiplies my chances for greater success. The only difference is that now I smile at rejections, but back in 2007, I used to be terrified by it. But you know the secret—however scared you are, however terrified you feel inside, go for it anyway. Your brave action in the face of fear will make you a legend.

This is why direct selling trainers are more powerful than any other kind of trainer. They have faced rejections and they have come to the stage by overcoming rejections and failures. Every rejection and ridicule you are facing today will give you applause and appreciation multiplied by 100 when you become successful and come to the stage.

My formula for fame and applause is simple:

Applause and appreciation you receive = 100 × rejection and ridicule you have endured.

A salesman minus enthusiasm is just another clerk.

–Harry F. Banks

Direct selling trains you not only for sales but also for success in life. This ability to handle failures is a phenomenal skill and it lies at the heart of success in any field. Once you develop it, you are set for life.

My immunity to rejections, my infinite ability to face a no, and my indomitable spirit in the face of challenges is the best gift this business has given me. I have been doing these three things, back to back, for more than thirteen years now—sell, grow and teach. This ongoing cycle of selling, growing and teaching, and then using this enhanced capability to sell more, grow more and teach the new things has put me on the path of a constant growth cycle and has been transforming me into a better version of myself every single day.

Meet me today, then come meet me after a few weeks—you will find a new version of me! I am doing it and loving it more with every passing day.

Direct Selling Income ≈ Number of Rejections You Will Face

Let me demonstrate to you the power of failure in building success through one simple example.

There was a pickle company named *Deepak Pickles*. They produced excellent pickles and sold 1000 bottles every month. They wanted to double their sales, so someone suggested they give an advertisement in the newspaper in a new location. They were sceptical about it, but still went ahead and did it. The newspaper had a circulation of 1,00,000 copies. Out of 1,00,000 people who got that newspaper, only 10,000 (only 10 per cent of people) saw their advertisement. Out of 10,000 who saw the advertisement, 90 per cent decided not to buy and only 1000 people bought a bottle of *Deepak Pickles*.

The *Deepak Pickles* advertisement failed 99 per cent as only 1000 out of 1,00,000 purchased the pickle bottles. But the company achieved their target 100 per cent and doubled their sales. Their goal was to sell 1000 extra pickle bottles and they achieved it.

Keep your focus on your goal and don't worry about the failures. Master communication and selling skills and fly to the top.

Practice is just as valuable as a sale. The sale will make you a living; the skill will make you a fortune.

–Jim Rohn

11

Start Your Own Business with Zero Risk

To build wealth today, you must be in your own business.

–John Getty

Many people want to start their own business, but two things hold them back:

1. High set-up cost
2. Fear of losing it all

For most regular businesses, you need the following to get started:

1. Office or working space
2. Infrastructure to run operations
3. Stock, if you are dealing in a product-based business
4. Reliable suppliers or vendors
5. Working capital to run operations
6. Quality manpower
7. Surplus funds for future contingencies

8. Marketing/advertising expertise and budget
9. Set-up for handling taxation and other statutory requirements
10. Training and development system for staff

All the above need a lot of money and management capability depending on the scale of the business you are planning to start. Most people don't have these things and hence they are not able to start the business.

The good news is that you don't need any of these to start direct selling. It's a home-based business that doesn't need office, staff, infrastructure, working capital, advertising, etc. There is a training and support system already in place to help you build your business. So you can start your own business at practically zero set-up cost.

Even if somebody can arrange to make available all the ten requirements listed above, the bigger challenge is how to generate cash flow and bring in sales. All these ten things are useless if you cannot generate enough sales. Managing the different aspects of business itself takes so much time that, often, new business owners are not able to devote enough time to sales.

In a direct selling business, all these ten set-up requirements are managed by the parent company, and your job is only to generate sales and develop a team that promotes products. When 100 per cent of your focus and time is going into sales, the chances of your success are naturally higher.

If you don't design your own life plan, chances are you will fall into someone else's plan. And guess what they have planned for you? Not much.

–Jim Rohn

For those of you who doubt whether direct selling is a legitimate business, just consider the constituents of any business:

- ✓ There is a manufacturer
- ✓ There is a seller
- ✓ There is a buyer
- ✓ There is a genuine product or service that is sold through a proper distribution model
- ✓ Profits or commissions are earned only on the sale of a product
- ✓ All taxes are paid as per government rules

All these elements are present in a direct selling business. Genuine products are sold and commissions are given after sale of products as per a pre-defined income model. No product can go from the factory to consumers without a set of middlemen. The traditional business marketing model has Carrying & Forwarding (C&F), a wholesaler, distributor, retailer, selling agent, etc., while the direct selling model has distributors. Just as most product distribution companies operate with a network of franchise stores, a direct selling business operates with a network of franchised individuals who are referred to as private franchisees by some authors.

The business model itself has been tried and proven successful worldwide for more than 50 years. It works for anyone who is willing to invest the necessary sweat equity required by any business.

–Brian Tracy

The beauty of direct selling is that it has made available to average individuals like you and me the power to build our own business and be an entrepreneur.

There is another common misconception that sometimes comes in the way of accepting that direct selling is a business. We have all been brought up to believe that you run a business only when you invest money and own assets, but that ideology is obsolete now. Of course, money is important, but your idea is more important than money in order to start a business. Facebook is one of the largest content creators in the world without writing a single piece of content themselves. Airbnb is one of the largest accommodation providers without owning a room. Uber is the world's largest taxi operator without owning most of their taxis.

Direct selling is an amazing opportunity for each and every individual to start their own business at zero set-up cost. It is entrepreneurship with total freedom and peace of mind.

If somebody offers you an amazing opportunity but you are not sure you can do it, say yes, then learn how to do it later.

–Richard Branson

12

A Great Nation-Building Service

Ask not what your country can do for you—ask what you can do for your country.

–John F. Kennedy

A nation is made up of its people. If any industry or business works towards empowering people to become contributing citizens with ideal values, then it is engaged in a great nation-building service. Some of the key contributions of the direct selling industry towards nation building are:

- Building an entrepreneurial culture by providing easy entrepreneurship options.
- Skill building of people through constant training and mentoring.
- Generating employment by giving equal opportunity to all.
- Paying taxes—every transaction in the business of direct selling is accounted for and tax is paid on the same.
- Providing moral education that builds a culture of people helping people.
- Helping in improving the per capita income of people.

As per a FICCI and KPMG joint report—DIRECT 2016—published in 2016 in India, the direct selling industry has contributed towards building India through activity in a big way in five major focus areas: Skill India, Make in India, Start-up India, Women Empowerment and Digital India. This report offers statistics on how direct selling has helped in all these projects.

As per another FICCI and KPMG report, 1.8 crore Indians are expected to be part of the Indian direct selling industry by 2025. Majority of these people will get ongoing training on leadership, sales, personality development, values, communication skills, character building, money management, and many other topics. All the income that these distributors earn will be tax-paid income. I consider it to be a good contribution in nation building.

I look at the direct selling business as a very democratic way to become rich. One rich and successful network marketer creates thousands of other rich and successful network marketers. It's a revolutionary way to entrepreneurship that can foster financial abundance in our society.

All the wealth of the world cannot help one little village if the people are not taught to help themselves. Our work should be mainly educational, both moral and intellectual.

–Swami Vivekananda

13
Reclaim Your Freedom

Freedom is the oxygen of the soul.

–Moshe Dayan

My first reason behind starting a direct selling business was of course money. During my first few years in the business, while sharing my experience, I used to quote five reasons why I started this business: Money, money, money, some more money, and still some more money. I had faced money scarcity throughout my formative years. I had studied on loans and had been taught to postpone my desires because we didn't have enough money. I was tired of always choosing only one from three toys or shirts that I loved. I desperately wanted financial abundance for my family and myself.

I wanted to pay off all my loans and wanted to live my dream lifestyle. I wanted to be debt-free and cash rich. But as I progressed in building this business, I realized the real game was not money; it was freedom. Today, after thirteen years in the business, I find myself even more excited about direct selling than ever before and the key reason for this is the freedom that a direct selling business offers to anyone.

Just imagine how exhilarating it is when, every single time I go to live events, I meet people who tell me they are in my team and have been doing business worth lakhs of rupees, month on month. Imagine my business system, wherein, every single day, I have more partners than I did yesterday, and I have not given sales presentations to any of them; I don't even know them! I am in the Bahamas on a cruise, or flying over the Grand Canyon in a private chartered aircraft with my family, while my business empire is multiplying. Believe me, I never imagined a life like this even in my wildest dreams, but direct selling made it possible for me.

If you don't like wherever you are, move; you are not a tree.

–Jim Rohn

First and foremost, freedom comes from the fact that anyone can start this business. You just need three things to start this business:

1. Dreams
2. Willingness to learn
3. Commitment to work for your dreams in a systematic way

A direct selling business offers you absolute freedom in choosing all the what, how, when, etc., of your business. It's you who will decide the following:

- When will you work and what will be your working hours?
- Whom will you choose to work with?
- Where will you build this business?
- What will be your style when building this business?
- How much income do you want to earn every month?
- What will you do with your income?

It's phenomenal and it sounds like a dream come true. You decide your working hours, your partners, your location, your work schedule and the income you want to earn. I must say this is one business that is truly built on your own terms.

Once you build this business correctly, you choose how you will spend your family time, you choose which hobbies you want to pursue, your lifestyle, your car, your vacations and, most importantly, whom you will spend your time with. Nowadays, there are so many other business models available as well that allow you to work with total freedom.

The only thing you need is to believe it first and then allow yourself the permission to make the necessary shift. Many of us didn't choose the career that we have today; our parents, teachers, seniors, neighbours, a counsellor, or some set of circumstances did this for us. But that time is gone. You can make a shift now. Interestingly, most of us don't need anybody's permission to make a career shift today. We just need to exercise this power to choose how we intend to live for the rest of our lives.

Either I will find a way, or I will make one.

–Philip Sidney

Way back in 2008, I went to meet a reputed chartered accountant (CA) in Chandigarh, India, to share our business opportunity. He was super successful in his career and was not really interested in anything I had to say. Suddenly, his sixteen-year-old son came to his chamber and proposed some idea that his father instantly rejected. I asked him, 'Why did you reject your son's idea?' He replied, 'What does a sixteen-year-old child know about life, career and decisions. He is too immature to take a decision.'

So I casually asked him when he decided to choose to be a CA by profession. He told me he decided when he passed his Class Ten examinations. I asked him what his age was at that time. 'Fifteen years,' he said. Then I asked him, 'You are not allowing your sixteen-year-old son to take this small decision, but imagine you made a decision to be a CA thirty years ago, when you were only fifteen! What did you know about career and life at that age? That decision was good at that point of time, but you need not continue with that decision for the rest of your life. You might not have had many options at that time, but now with all the knowledge, maturity and wisdom you have, you can make better choices and make the rest of your life the best of your life.'

So, if you are one of those who want to live the rest of your life with total and absolute freedom, you can consider direct selling a worthwhile career option. Remember, the goal is not money. The goal is freedom.

There is no greater freedom than the freedom to be yourself. Give yourself that gift and choose to surround yourself with those who appreciate you exactly as you truly are.

–Doe Zantamata

14

The Best Career Enhancement Tool for Students

What you learn in your college will give you a career; what you learn on the streets will give you life and lifestyle.

–Deepak Bajaj

Our colleges and universities are slowly evolving towards providing a holistic education, but, primarily, what they continue to teach students are conventional, core subjects. To be successful in your career, you need much more than just subject knowledge. You need work skills that will bring more results and productivity. Along with these work skills, you need life skills, and the irony is that no college or university is teaching those skills.

This is where direct selling can play a significant role. Direct selling can supplement college education by imparting all essential work skills and life skills needed to facilitate overall development that will empower every student to lead a good life.

Here are ten key benefits that direct selling would impart to students:

1. **Make them financially self-reliant**

   Students can earn their own pocket money and be financially self-reliant at an early age.

2. **Real-life experience that adds value to their resume**

   Everyone gets a degree, but what makes a difference is real-life experience. A student with experience easily stands out from the rest. Direct selling can give this edge and make students more employable.

3. **Self-confidence**

   Developing confidence is a process, and there are some things that can really help in enhancing a student's self-confidence—new learning, earning, meeting new people, work, among others. Direct selling provides all of these and many more benefits to students and can polish their personality and confidence levels.

4. **Time management and self-discipline**

   How you manage your 24-hour-day determines the level of your success. A direct selling business will empower students to learn how to manage their time better.

5. **Real-life entrepreneurial education and experience**

   This is a priceless gain, and many entrepreneurs lose huge sums of money and time owing to lack of the right kind of entrepreneurial experience. Without any major investment and risk, students get a chance to actually live like an entrepreneur while pursuing their education.

6. **Learn to manage their money better**

   When you earn money, your attitude towards money changes. You start valuing it much more. Students who can gain this experience early in life will eventually manage their money better.

7. **People skills**

   People skills are what students will need the most in their job, profession, or business, and direct selling makes them master people skills.

8. **Decision-making ability**

   Decision-making ability is a key requisite for success in any field, and direct selling empowers you in terms of correct decision making.

9. You build your professional network

Your network is your actual net worth. Direct selling offers unlimited opportunity to students to expand their professional network. This network will be their biggest asset in their career.

10. Opportunity to learn new skills

Everyday is a learning day when you are building your direct selling business. Your college will teach you academics and direct selling will teach you life skills and work skills. This combination can take your career to the next level.

I highly recommend that every student pursues a part-time direct selling business alongside their studies. A few years in direct selling can totally transform a student, propelling them ahead much faster in their chosen career. I am seeing a huge shift in the attitude and mindset of students. An impressive number of them are reading my books and following my social media channels. So many students come for my workshops and take up my online courses to supplement their college studies. This keen urge to grow is a good sign, and I am glad to serve the student community in such huge numbers.

Learning is not the product of teaching. Learning is the product of the activity of learners.

–John Holt

15
Real Insurance and Security for Your Family

At the end of the day, the goals are simple: safety and security.

–Jodi Rell

When I was six, my father was diagnosed with a fatal disease. He spent the next two years mostly in the hospital. My mother provided for the best medical care possible in those days. At the end of those two years, we lost our dad, and all the savings and assets that he had accumulated with his government job as well. All our relatives also disappeared. It took more than two years for my mother to get a job. Those were the toughest years of our lives and we learnt so many lessons.

My father was the most awesome human being I know. He was a great social worker, and the whole village used to come to him when they needed any sort of help. But he didn't anticipate this situation; probably nobody does. Everything was wonderful for us as long as he was alive, but once he was gone, gone were our family's monthly income, assets, and all our friends and relatives. Every single day of those tough years remains etched in my heart. It taught me that during our working years, we should set up a mechanism that will continue to provide an income to our family when we are no longer able to work, or even after we are gone.

A great chunk of families have only one earning member, and during their golden years, that person refuses to accept that, one day, he or she may not be able to work any more due to some medical condition or tragedy. So how will the family maintain the same lifestyle when the person stops working? It's easy to upgrade our lifestyle when things are going well, but it's very difficult to manage when the things we have become used to are taken away; it becomes tough to survive without them.

Go for it now. The future is promised to no one.

–Wayne Dyer

Insurance agents scare us and use such stories to make us buy their policies, but the fact remains that one lump sum insurance amount cannot take care of our family for the rest of their lives. I am not saying it is not good. You must cover yourselves adequately with insurance. But I want to point out that it's not enough. You need an ongoing income stream that will continue to bring in income even without your active involvement or presence. You need a business that will work without you, generation after generation, one with a nomination facility. The faster you realize this truth, the quicker you will look for solutions. And my job is to make you understand its importance well before such a situation may actually arise in your life.

You can choose to achieve this by building a traditional business. But even after decades of work, only a handful of people are able to take their business to this height. We have already discussed the challenges in starting a traditional business. Even if you build one successfully, it is so complex and demands such levels of competency, expertise and management skills, that it would be very difficult for your spouse or kids to run the business and keep it profitable.

I am sure you have heard the story about a frog in boiling water. If a frog is suddenly thrown into boiling water, it will immediately jump out of it. But if the frog is thrown into lukewarm water, which is then boiled slowly, it will not perceive the impending danger and will be boiled to death. In the second case, the frog understands that there is a slight challenge, and uses all its energy in managing the situation. So the water keeps getting hotter and the frog keeps using more and more of its energy in managing it, rather than jumping out of it. When the temperature becomes unbearably hot, there is no energy left in the frog to make the jump, and it dies. What brought death to this good frog were two things:

1. The inability or unwillingness to recognize danger in time
2. Inaction when it had time and resources to act

In this respect, I strongly believe direct selling is a nomination-based business in the true sense of the term, one that is available to each and every common person. Here, when the main person who is building the business is no more there, the entire business income will be transferred to the dependents or nominee.

The most amazing thing about a direct selling business is the system that drives the business, and not the individual. The core philosophy of this model is to develop and empower thousands of people through a system of tools, training and events in such a way that a large number of people create a small volume each. Since every individual is handling only a small volume and there are large numbers of individuals engaged in the work, business is not dependent on the presence, competency, skills or expertise of any one particular individual. Moreover, every good direct selling company and team has a highly evolved system of tools, training and events that keeps people active and productive.

If you build this business with the right foundation and system, not only will your children's lives be taken care of, but when you grow old, you too will not be dependent on anyone to take care of you. Once you build a direct selling business, it will take care of you till your last breath.

The richest people in the world build networks. Everyone else is trained to look for work.

–Robert T. Kiyosaki

16

Catalyst in Your Career Promotion and Professional Growth

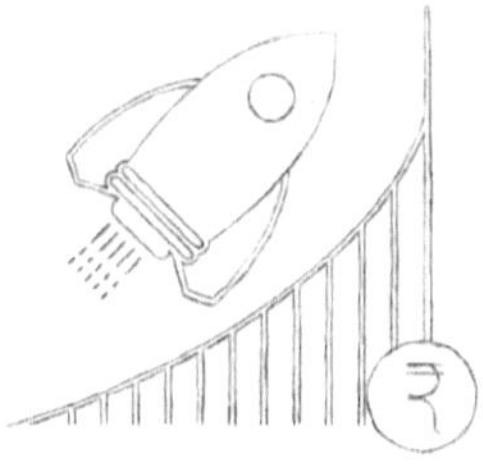

Don't go through life; grow through life.

–Eric Butterworth

Whatever the profession or position, there is one thing every one of us is seeking, and that is growth. Everyone wants a better job, higher position, more income, more recognition and better status. In fact, this is what drives people at work. Which is probably why appraisal time is considered to be most critical in every organization.

Fundamentally, there are two things that determine your position, salary or professional fees—education and work experience. These are the parameters you are checked on during the interview. Generally speaking, people with better degrees and more experience get a better title, more salary, and can charge higher professional fees.

Although everyone wants promotion and growth, most people just stop learning after they have graduated from college, and they don't pursue any new educational course or learn any enhanced skills to really qualify for the promotion. How can you ask for a better salary for doing the same job in the same way with the same set of knowledge, skills and experience?

Please also remember that good academic and professional skills are easily found today. Everyone has a degree, and a degree can only get you started in a career, but if you want to outgrow everyone else, you need skills beyond mere degrees.

Regular degrees + basic skills = Regular salary and position

Regular degrees + new education + special skills
= Big promotions and big increments

The rule is simple: If you keep doing the same things in the same old ways, you will keep getting the same old rewards and benefits. If you need a better income, position and status, you need to change yourself and work on making yourself better.

Both of us recommend a part-time direct selling business as another means of gaining leadership training. These opportunities force you to meet and communicate with people. This is a tough thing for many people, but is an absolute requirement for success. It's better to stretch when the stakes are low than to do it when your life depends on it. People skills are not optional. They are absolutely required for success.

–Donald Trump and Robert Kiyosaki

There are a number of ways to acquire further education and relevant experience, and you can choose the one that seems to work best for you. But with my thirteen years of intensive, full-time direct selling experience, I can firmly say that building a direct selling business prepares you really well for the highest kind of growth in your job/ profession. It teaches you skills that are absolutely essential for growth in any career. In fact, direct selling not only teaches you but also trains you in such a way that these extraordinary skills become a part of you.

In a direct selling business, people are the only available resource, and only capable people can do better business. Hence, there is a huge emphasis on developing people. Every good direct selling company and team works with a powerful training and development system.

Direct selling training programmes and fieldwork train you in the following areas:

- ✓ Sales
- ✓ Interpersonal communication
- ✓ Building teams
- ✓ Leadership

- ✓ Personality development
- ✓ Time management
- ✓ Public speaking
- ✓ Motivating and leading teams
- ✓ Influence and charisma
- ✓ Right attitude and beliefs
- ✓ People management

These skills are rare to find and priceless once found. Every employer or boss is desperately looking for these skills in people, and once you develop them, you will be unstoppable in your career.

So, if we look beyond the income and lifestyle that a direct selling business provides, anyone who wants to develop any of the skills mentioned above for growth in their job or profession should consider direct selling.

Growth is painful. Change is painful. But in the end, nothing is as painful as staying stuck somewhere you do not belong.

–Mandy Hale

17

Tax Advantages

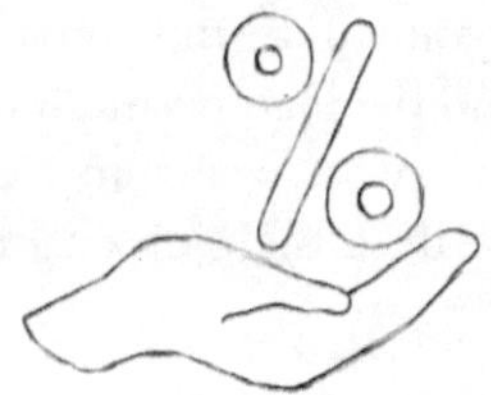

The only thing worse than paying income tax is not having an income to pay tax on.

–Deepak Bajaj

Broadly speaking, three things remain permanent aspects of our income—we earn money, spend money and pay taxes. Everyone does these three things, but the sequence in which they are done varies among employees and business owners.

If you are an employee, you earn money and then pay taxes. Most of the taxes are deducted as TDS (Tax Deducted at Source) even before you are paid your salary. So the formula for an employee is simple: Earn money, pay taxes, and spend the leftover. Also, being an employee, you cannot claim any deductions from your income other than a finite amount of a few specified expenses.

But a business owner is allowed to deduct all the expenses that have been incurred in the process of building the business. It is assumed that since you are generating revenue, you must be incurring some expenses in the process of generating that revenue. These are called deductible expenses. There is a wide range of deductible expenses, and as a business owner, you are allowed to deduct these expenses from your income before you pay your taxes. A part or the total of some basic expenses that you have already been incurring, such as home office rent, car loan interest, car fuel cost, maintenance costs, laptop, mobile, Internet, stationery, travel, dining, hotels, etc., can qualify as deductible expenses once you start a business. The important thing, of course, is first to have a legitimate business, and then to incur expenses that fall under the definition of deductible expenses as per applicable tax laws. So the formula for a businessperson is: Earn money, deduct all the expenses incurred, and pay taxes on the leftover.

In summary, this equation works thus:

For employees: Income – Taxes
= Amount available for expenses and lifestyle

For business persons: Income – Expenses
= Pay taxes on the leftover

Businesses are the key drivers of the economy that create jobs and generate money. I assume this tax advantage must be given to business owners to encourage more people to start a business and to empower business owners to engage in more activities in order to generate maximum revenue. When you build a direct selling business, your income is considered to be business income, and you are entitled to all the benefits that any regular business owner enjoys. When a privilege is given to you, why not take benefit of it?

So it goes without saying that all this will be applicable when you run a legitimate business as per prevailing laws, and all the deductions will be allowed as per provisions specified. All the information given here is an example of a few possibilities, but you need to consult your tax lawyers and consultants for more details and best provisions available for your current situation.

Fundamentally, whatever tax advantages are available to any business owner will also be available to a direct selling business owner, as long as they are able to prove that these expenses have been incurred for the enhancement of the business.

Change the way you make money if you want to change the amount of taxes you pay.

–Diane Kennedy

18
Develop Life Skills for a Better Life

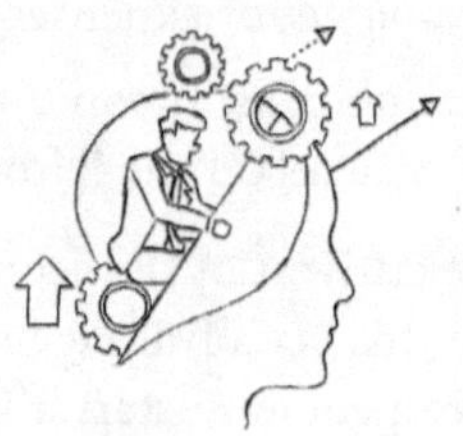

Build your skills, not your resume.

–Sheryl Sandberg

Our schools and universities teach us skills to secure a job or profession. This education is great, but it's limited to knowledge and skills related to work. Work is only a part of life, though, and we need other skills to grow and flourish in life. Academic and technical skills can get you started with a job, but to really grow in your career, you need several other skills as well. When you start building your direct selling business, it gradually starts developing in you many life skills that will empower you to live a happy, successful and prosperous life.

Some of the essential life skills you develop in the process of building a direct selling business are as follows:

- Handling rejection
- Patience
- Dealing with people
- Optimism
- Goal-setting
- Crisis management

- Perseverance
- Enthusiasm
- Constant learning
- Adaptability to change
- Self-discipline
- Stress management
- Confidence
- Consistency
- Punctuality
- Money management
- Emotional resilience
- Building and nurturing relationships

Building your skill set is the sure shot way to go to the top. When you build your skills, you enhance your value. My daughter once asked me, 'Dad, why do people pay thousands of rupees to attend your workshops and lakhs of rupees for your coaching?' I told her it's because I give them value for the money they invest with me. It is a simple life philosophy—you will be paid purely based on the value you deliver. The cup of tea that is available for ten rupees at a roadside tea stall is sold for a few hundred rupees in a five-star hotel. The price you can charge for your product or services depends entirely on the value you deliver.

You want to be paid more in your job/profession? Simply become more valuable. How can you be more valuable? By enhancing your knowledge and skill set. Go for it. Every hour invested in your growth and development always gives the highest returns on investment.

The key to success is to keep growing in all areas of life—mental, emotional, spiritual as well as physical.

–Julius Erving

19

Fame and Recognition

The deepest principle in human nature is the craving to be appreciated.

–William James

Recognition and appreciation are basic human needs. Recognition comes from excellence in your work and it converts into fame when your excellence scales new heights and impacts a larger number of people. Generally speaking, people with extraordinary skills in any field find a chance to enjoy fame and recognition, but what I admire about direct selling is the fact that it provides opportunity, a supporting system and conducive environment that can empower and enable any common person to achieve fame and recognition.

Moreover, when you rise to the top in direct selling, it's never an individual victory but a team accomplishment. You just cannot rise to the top in direct selling without creating a big number of achievers in your team. The fame and recognition you receive for your success is fundamentally recognition of your contribution in the betterment of many other people's lives. To me, that is the best way to achieve fame and recognition. It's really incredible to be honoured and remembered for the good work you have done for others.

My home is full of trophies and mementos. I have hundreds of them; there is a whole wall dedicated to displaying them, and whatever has not found place on that huge wall has been kept in my library and in several other places in my villa. Each of these trophies represents lakhs of people whom I have influenced while building my direct selling business empire, and these mementos continue to inspire me everyday as I passionately pursue my mission to empower more and more people to fulfil their dreams and to live their best lives.

How many houses have you visited where you found a trophy wall, and even those that have one mostly carrythe prizes the kids won in school. Why should this trend stop at school? Why should our achievements end with college or university? Why should we stop pursuing excellence in whatever we do? Every day in our life is an opportunity to add value and contribute to the well-being of others. Let's use the opportunity and let's rise by lifting others. Recognition also uplifts our own self-image.

I am not saying that if you don't win a trophy, you are not living a good life. What I am proposing is to live life in such a way that a part of your life is dedicated to uplifting other human beings, and when you do that, you will receive genuine recognition and ever-growing fame.

Your profession is not what brings home your weekly pay check; your profession is what you are put here on earth to do, with such passion and such intensity that it becomes spiritual in calling.

–Vincent Van Gogh

There's another thing. Please know that there is nothing wrong in aspiring for fame and recognition. Why not aspire for a life where you don't need to introduce yourself anymore? In fact, recognition multiplies your circle of influence and allows you to spread your good work to more and more number of people. Look at the celebrities in our midst and see how they use their fame and recognition for so many noble causes and become a change agent.

Fame per se is not good or bad; it's all about how you handle it. There are innumerable people in history who rose to fame and then fell to ashes because of their inability and weakness to handle that position. For me, direct selling has not only given fame and recognition but the character, humility and responsibility to handle it and leverage it to expand the good work I have been doing. It has become an asset which helps me do even more good. Thanks to the fame and recognition that the direct selling industry has given me, I am now able to contribute much more and much faster towards making this world a better place.

Currently, people from 100+ countries have been attending my training sessions and online courses, reading my books or watching my free training videos, and this number is multiplying by the minute. The root cause behind this is that I respect my fans, readers, subscribers and students. I have been working with the principle that whatever time and money they are investing with me should give them back at least ten times that value. Every video in my online courses and every page in my book has been created with the intention of bringing instant change and lasting transformation. I want to bring results to people and solve their problems faster.

I work obsessively to create new training modules, tools and techniques to make success easier and faster to obtain for people. My life mission is to impact and empower more and more people every single day through my workshops, training events, professional talks, online courses, books, free video trainings, free eBooks and social media channels. The biggest reward is not my collection of cars or properties or bank balance, but the positive contribution I am able to make in people's lives.

Fame is the perfume of heroic deeds.

–Socrates

20

Empowering Your Friends and Social Circle

Align yourself with people that you can learn from, people who want more out of life, people who are stretching and searching and seeking higher grounds in life.

–Les Brown

Everyone is familiar with the slogan: Your company determines your destiny. We have likely heard this throughout our growing up years. My teachers always used to say, birds of the same feather flock together. My parents and teachers used this maxim to keep me away from my classmates who used to smoke, drink, or those who were not good in studies. I remained under the impression that the role of this philosophy was limited to that age and stage. But as time progressed, I realized that the size of our achievements throughout life is directly proportional to the kind of people with whom we closely associate.

This effect is gradual and powerful, to the extent that, after a point, it becomes so intense that we don't even realize we are affected by it. We get used to it and we start looking at mediocrity and compromise as normal. Since everyone around us lives a similar life, we start accepting things and stop questioning anything. What's worse is that if you are the best person in a group, you are finished. You get so much admiration from people around you that you start feeling that you have reached the top. The moment your group makes you feel that you have reached the top—that is the end of your dreams. I have personally faced this several times in my life, but every time I pulled myself out of that circle, it was a big career jump for me.

During my High Performance Coaching sessions, one of the things I specifically work on with my clients is fixing their inner circles and building systems and strategies to create an environment where success becomes automatic for them.

Consider it similar to walking into a newly painted home. For the first day, the smell of the paint is unbearable. It may be so overpowering that you vomit, and you may not be able to eat food all day in that house. With every passing day, you start adjusting to the smell and, after a point, you even stop noticing it. When an outsider visits your home, the smell of paint is so bad that he questions you, 'How can you live in a house with such a strong smell!' Now you start wondering what is wrong with this person. Where is the smell?

Please remember, wherever you are today is the effect of your friends and people with whom you closely associate—your inner circle. Your finances, your health, your relationships, your assets, your career and the quality of your life are greatly influenced by your circle.

You are the average of the five people you spend the most time with.

–Jim Rohn

So if you intend to make a change in the financial area (or any other area) of your life, you need to immediately change your friends and social circle. I invite you for a ten-minute exercise right now. Take the role of your coach. Become your own coach for the next ten minutes and just evaluate who are the people whom you regularly meet and spend time with. Use the sheet given at the end of this chapter or use your own notebook and start writing down their names. Start with yesterday, and write down the names of everyone you met or spoke on the phone with, yesterday. Just keep going back one day at a time, and start noticing the people with whom you spend most of your time over the phone or in person. Just go over the last two weeks for this exercise.

Now evaluate their lives on different parameters that are important to you—money, health, relationships, career, etc. Just see how your thoughts, lifestyle and achievements have many things in common.

If you find merit in whatever I am saying, I urge you to start making a shift right now in your inner circle. I am not asking you to end your relationships with your friends, but the key is to spend more time with those who empower you and whose lifestyle you want to achieve and adopt. Identify people whom you want in your circle and find ways of spending more time with them. Continue your efforts and remember it's a slow and subtle process. The results will be visible over time.

You cannot change the people around you, but you can change the people you choose to be around.

–Unknown

With my personal experience, I can guarantee you that there will come a time when things that once gave you pleasure may start feeling like punishment. Some of the people with whom you were really comfortable may appear suffocating. The things you used to tolerate and even enjoy will suddenly start irritating you. Your choice of words will change. Your expectations from yourself and your life will change and that will pave the way for a new life for you.

If you have never experienced it, I invite you to make a shift and experience it for yourself right from today. If you don't like your new friends, you can always go back to your old friends and old ways of life. I urge you to make an attempt. Many a times, I have seen people attend a training programme or read a book and then initiate change in their lives. One of the reasons why they can't make changes and go back to their old self is their friends and close circle.

Some of you feel that you are so positive in life that nothing will happen to you. It's a myth. Every word you allow to get into your mind is like a seed, and these seeds will become plants and trees at some point of time. You may guard yourself from outsiders, but your friends and others in your social circle slowly affect you in such a way that you don't even realize the damage possibly being done.

This ability to determine whom you should listen to and whom you should avoid is a million-dollar skill. Many people with high potential and excellent capabilities are not growing in life because they are listening to the wrong people. Direct selling will silently develop this incredible ability in you to determine whom you should really listen to.

Let me remind you of a valuable story.

There was once a competition among frogs to climb the tallest tower of the village. Many daring frogs accepted the challenge while hundreds of others gathered to witness the race. Frogs are great at jumping and hopping from one place to the other, but climbing up a tall tower needs a different skill. At the sound of the whistle, many participants started climbing. As soon as the participants started climbing, many frogs in the crowd started shouting—'That tower is too high. You will fall off and die. Frogs can never climb towers. You will never make it to the top. If you fall from this height you will break your bones. You can't do it. Are you crazy?' As the crowd predicted, many frogs began to fall. The crowd continued to shout and frogs kept falling off, one after the other. Despite jeering from the crowd, one tiny frog continued undeterred on his way upwards.

The crowd was shocked to see this tiny frog make it to the top. They were amazed and bewildered. They were curious to know how this tiny frog made it to the top when everybody else had failed. So the moment he got down, they started asking him how he did it. The tiny frog was silent. Everyone was asking questions, but he didn't reply to anyone. Suddenly a mamma frog came running and said, 'Stop bothering my child. He is deaf. He cannot hear.' The only reason this tiny frog could reach the top was because he never listened to what the crowd said.

Associate with people of vision. Be around those who inspire you and motivate you to reach your dreams.

–Joel Osteen

Born in a government employee's family in a small town, I never had access to people from rich, business communities. We grew up surrounded by people who were like us. The difference between rich and middle-class people lies not just in money and lifestyle but principally in their thought process and in how they look at opportunities and situations in life. Our definition of a good life was based on concepts such as budgeting, cutting expenses, job security, adjustment, compromise, sacrifice, living within means, saving, luxuries are a crime, rich people are cheats, and so on. With every passing day, this philosophy became more deeply ingrained in our thinking and gradually became a part of us. The worst damage this kind of thinking does is to kill growth mentality and fighting spirit.

If you look at the people in your circle and you don't get inspired, then you don't have a circle. You have a cage.

–Nipsey Hussle

For years, I tried to get over this mentality. I knew I wanted to change my friends, but working in a regular job, I did not know how to find a positive and empowering environment every single day of my life. I couldn't imagine how to get access to people who are committed to their dreams and have been on a growth mission.

Then in 2007, there came the chance to get into direct selling. Direct selling gave me the set of friends I was looking for—people who were on the same mission as I was. People who didn't just discuss change but actually worked to make a change—ordinary human beings with extraordinary commitment. Passionate, optimistic, high-dreaming, committed hard workers who knew where they were going and were relentlessly working towards their goals. This circle slowly started shifting my beliefs, then my thinking, and finally my habits and behaviour.

One of the reasons why people run away when someone approaches them with the idea of direct selling is their childhood conditioning which is a result of continued association. For most of their lives, people have been surrounded by employees, self-employed individuals, or professionals. People hear stories and watch videos of successful businessmen and businesswomen, but they hardly get a chance to be around someone who has built a business in the true sense of it.

Business owners don't just have different financial statements; they also have entirely different values and life philosophies. The world of business runs on possibilities and opportunities, while a majority of people keep looking for security and guarantees. So when a direct selling business opportunity comes along, they look to escape because it just doesn't match their life values. But if you genuinely want to build a big business, you need to develop that kind of a value system. Direct selling gives you unlimited access to people with business values and a business mindset.

Direct selling not only provides a great business education, it also provides a whole-new world of friends—friends who are going in the same direction as you are and share the same core values as you.

–Robert T. Kiyosaki

The biggest gift of direct selling is a set of empowering friends who pull you up. Friends who celebrate your success and always inspire you to carry on. People with a shared mission are the biggest force on earth, and direct selling empowered me with this great army of friends who propelled me to greater heights of success every single day. In my job too, I had so many friends who claimed to be my well-wishers, but I soon realized that they were friends not to me but to the position I was holding in the company. And they remained friends so long as I didn't get a promotion.

Some people feel that relationships are ruined in the process of direct selling, but to tell you the truth—relationships are not ruined but tested in this field. The moment you announce that you have started this business, the very same people who once appreciated you will change colours and start saying things like, 'This business doesn't suit you, it won't work…', 'You have made a huge mistake, you will lose everything in this business…', 'You have gone mad!' and so on.

The psychology at play behind this is their fear of being left behind. They fear that you may get ahead, and they will do everything it takes to pull you down so that you stay at their level. Once you grow, they will also have to grow to retain your friendship, and the truth is—they don't want to grow. So the best alternative is to do everything they can to ensure that you don't grow either. Many people quit at this stage and sabotage this amazing transformative process of becoming a totally new human being.

There is a classic story of red crabs. Once, there was a big ship that did the job of catching crabs from the sea. All the crabs that were caught were kept in plastic crates. All the crates were sealed with a lid, except for a few huge crates. A new trainee on the ship asked the captain, 'All the crates are duly sealed with lids, but these few crates are left open. These crabs can easily run away to the sea, wasting our efforts.' The captain replied, 'These are red crabs. The moment one crab tries to run away, the other crabs pull it back. They will never be able to run away.'

The hidden benefit of a direct selling business is the unlimited access to financially free people who are willing to help you achieve financial abundance. In this world of cut-throat competition, imagine a business model wherein people who are senior to you in the business mentor you and share every single business secret with you, so that you can achieve the same amount of success as they have. To me, this is the best possible company or association on earth.

The key is to keep company only with people who uplift you, whose presence calls forth your best.

–Epictetus

Your Inner Circle Evaluation Sheet

Name	Monthly Income	Car	Quality of Life

21
Continuous Personal Growth

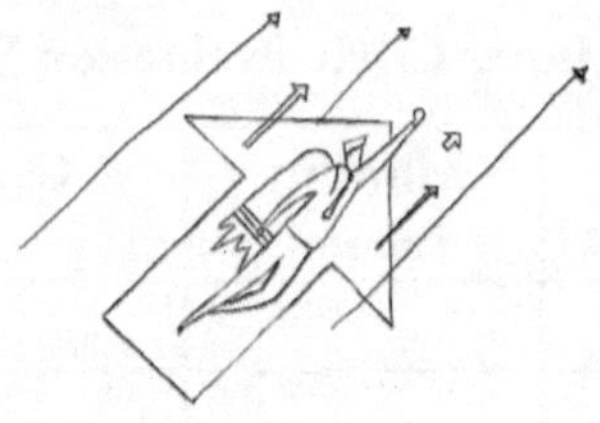

Growing old is mandatory, growing up is optional.

–Chili Davis

One of the greatest gifts Nature bestows on human beings is the ability to grow and evolve. Zoology puts us humans in the same class as all other animals. But one thing that distinguishes us from other living beings is our ability to continuously grow and evolve. Only human beings have this unique feature; so anyone who does not utilize this gift is not fully utilizing the natural privileges of their human birth.

When I make these statements aloud, some people hide behind the pretext of 'satisfaction'. They proudly say, 'I am satisfied' or 'I am content'. And most times, this statement is used as an excuse to avoid doing something. You will generally find these two things go together—satisfaction and non-action. I call it the SNA (Satisfaction and Non-action) virus. If you too have been infected with this SNA virus, or there are people in your circle who have been infected with this virus, please read the following paragraph carefully, and re-read it if required.

A long time ago, everyone used to walk and run. People did not know of any form of transportation. Everyone was happy and satisfied, except one person who was not satisfied with walking and who believed there must be another way. This person invented the bicycle. Now all those satisfied people started enjoying the bicycle. Soon, everyone was satisfied with the bicycle, except one person who didn't enjoy the tiring process of pedalling the bicycle. This person believed there must be another way, and that dissatisfaction resulted in the invention of the motorcycle. Everyone now started enjoying motorcycles and was satisfied with this mode of transport, except one person who did not like being affected by rain, wind or sun while riding the motorcycle. This person continued to work hard and finally invented a car. This delighted everyone and the car became a popular vehicle. People were satisfied with the car, yet there was one person who wanted the car ride to be luxurious and ultra-comfortable. That dissatisfied person invented luxury automobiles. Naturally, everyone started enjoying the fruits of this person's labour. All were satisfied, except two brothers who believed there must be a faster way to travel. And by virtue of their dissatisfaction and relentless efforts, the airplane was created.

Please understand that everything we enjoy today, be it pen and paper, a laptop, an air-conditioned car, a centrally heated building, designer clothes, or any man-made article for the matter, has only come into existence because someone was not satisfied and put in hard work to improvise and build something new.

Think about it: Had Bhagat Singh, Mahatma Gandhi, and other freedom fighters stayed satisfied with British rule over India, you and I would have been born as slaves. This freedom our nation won was also the result of the toil of a few men and women who were not satisfied with living conditions in the land.

If you feel you are satisfied and don't need more, why don't you work to serve others and contribute to society. Why are you being selfish and lazy when your country and the world need your contribution?

I too believe in satisfaction. I believe in counting our blessings and being thankful for all that we have, but I am fiercely against sitting idle and making satisfaction an excuse for cowardice and laziness. Be satisfied with whatever you have, but use all your talent and resources to keep growing and contributing. Satisfaction should only make you work more with a smile on your face and contentment in your heart.

Growth is life and staying the same is death.

–Deepak Bajaj

Let me bring to your attention another beautiful thing about the nature of growth. A person can never grow in isolation. I just love this law of nature which dictates that when you grow, many others also grow with you. Your decision to grow and your commitment to do whatever it takes to grow will automatically uplift many other people, and that truly is the best aspect of growth.

I strongly believe that your growth is your duty. Your success is your obligation. Every new accomplishment of yours helps society in some way or the other and positively influences many others to chase their dreams. You set in motion a growth phenomenon that collectively uplifts humanity. Each one of us must grow, and this growth will then propel and inspire others around us to grow as well. In an ideal society, all individuals grow together as one community.

Growth is evidence that there is life. Keep growing. Work with an attitude that says: Either I will find a way or I will make a way, but whatever it is, I will keep moving.

If you can't fly, then run.
If you can't run, then walk.
If you can't walk, then crawl.
But by all means, keep moving.

–Martine Luther King Jr

Poor or middle-class people continue to struggle financially for no reason except that they have stopped growing in life. Most people stop learning new things after they pass out of college. People keep doing the same work for years on end at their jobs, dealing with the same kind of people and handling the same issues monotonously. The more time they spend in one particular job, the greater is their fear from anything outside and beyond that job.

This fear makes them blind to new opportunities. And what's worse is that when growth-oriented people approach them, they find excuses to run away. Every time they run away from big dreamers, they push themselves deeper into the mire of a life of poverty, compromise and more fear. This becomes a vicious cycle that prevents them from becoming rich and successful.

Direct selling with its continuous growth-oriented system pulls you out of this cycle and puts you on a new cycle of continuous growth and newer accomplishments. A direct selling business is like a school of life that empowers and inspires you to constantly keep growing by providing:

- ✓ Several opportunities for learning new knowledge and skills
- ✓ A conducive environment for learning
- ✓ The right support system that strengthens learning
- ✓ Constant motivation for new learning

If we don't change, we don't grow. If we don't grow, we are not living.

–Gail Sheehy

A direct selling system pushes you out of your comfort zone and forces you to stretch yourself to your limits. The best gift direct selling has given me was the environment that encouraged me to grow continually. I started my direct selling business in 2007, and as of 2020, when this book has been published, this attitude of continually testing my limits, growing, improving, and surprising myself with what more I can do is something for which I will always be grateful to direct selling.

I still remember starting this business in my 900 sq. ft. rented house on the second floor of a small home in Chandigarh. Today, I live in a villa spread over an area of more than 10,000 sq. ft., and I own three more houses. My first car bought from earnings from this business was a Maruti Alto worth 2 lakh rupees. Today, I have a collection of cars worth crores of rupees. Honestly speaking, I couldn't believe it when I bought my first Mercedes Benz in 2009, but today when I think of owning a private aircraft, my mind accepts it with absolute faith. This new belief system that direct selling gradually instilled in me is what makes me fall in love with this industry more and more with every passing day.

Villas, cars, bank balance, etc.—these are just an outwardly expression of what you are becoming every single day. These are trophies of your achievement and certificates of your growth. All these are worldly possessions, but what you became in the process of earning these things is priceless and stays with you forever. It's a true reflection of your mental and emotional growth. Growth is life, my dear friend, and I invite you today to start this journey of constant and never-ending growth.

Every new accomplishment draws more big dreamers to

you. Your circle becomes even more powerful and empowering, and all the high dreamers then motivate one other to accomplish even more.

I have adopted this idea of constant and never-ending growth from Tony Robbins. I have been to USA, Europe, Singapore, Bangkok, among other places, to attend training programmes conducted by some of the best trainers around the world. During a powerful live event in the USA, I experienced a shift in my beliefs and realized that we can completely change in one instant. I have been brought up with this belief that change is painful and takes time, but that one shift in my belief that I can change anytime I decide to change has put me on the path of an exponential growth journey. I invested close to ₹ 10 lakhs for that event, but I have earned much more because of the mind shift I gained in the process. I design all my workshops and online training courses to gift a similar mind shift to all my participants.

The direct selling business puts you on a growth cycle that I call the LDT cycle of continuous growth.

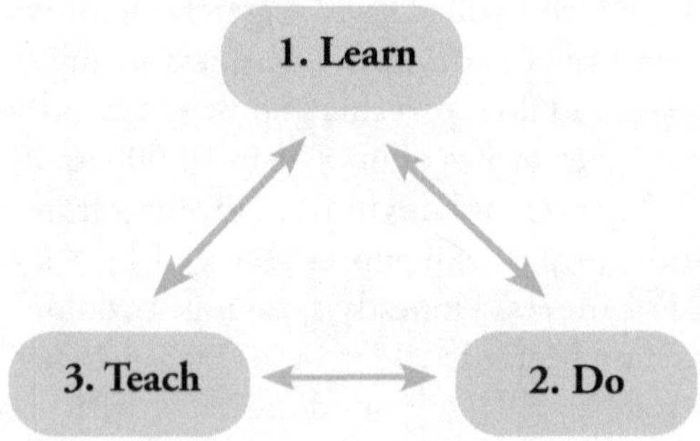

LDT cycle of continuous growth

Everybody starts off as a student in direct selling and learns new knowledge, tools, skills and techniques. You are then encouraged to use those skills and tools in the field. Learning strengthens by doing. With repeated learning and doing, you master those skills, and then teach those same skills to others. When you teach something, that further strengthens your own learning, and these new lessons learnt gradually become a part of you. This is the LDT cycle, and as you grow in the business, you keep learning new skills and tools.

In any given moment, we have two options: to step forward into growth or to step back into safety.

–Abraham Maslow

Direct selling builds your growth mindset by constantly exposing you to an environment that encourages and supports growth. The hidden boon of direct selling is the new environment that it gives you. Believe it or not, we all are a product of our environment. If you have the vision and the patience to stick with direct selling for a few years, the environment here will make you a different person.

There is another practical reason why I recommend people try direct selling. I know so many people who accept that they need to grow, but stay stuck in the same place for years. Their desire to grow remains a wish. This is because most people need a push and a constant reminder in order to grow. The direct selling system does exactly that. Learning and growing is not optional but necessary for survival and success in this field.

Many people who quit, saying that the business doesn't work, are actually the ones who were uncomfortable with the growth required and were not willing to grow. They wanted to build the business from their own comfort zone. To grow your direct selling business, you need to change, learn and grow. Most people are not willing to do that. There is so much positivity here that negative people just cannot handle it.

So if you have even the slightest inclination to grow and you are feeling stuck, consider building a direct selling business with a credible organization with a well-developed training and development system. Work with a good mentor, follow their system, and do what is advised. I am sure you will become a much better person.

Practise the philosophy of continuous improvement. Get a little bit better every single day.

–Brian Tracy

22
Zero-Risk Entrepreneurship Training

Entrepreneurship is neither a science nor an art. It is a practice.
–Peter Drucker

Entrepreneurship is in the air. Conceptually, it has been there since time immemorial, but the craze to be an entrepreneur that we have seen over the last two decades is unmatched. It's the number one buzzword now. Tons of people, students and employees alike want to take up entrepreneurship. Governments and various agencies are promoting it like never before, constantly working to create an ecosystem that supports entrepreneurship.

Yes, the number of entrepreneurs is on the rise. Yet, there are millions of people who want to be entrepreneurs but are not able to take a step forward in that direction. Here are the major reasons:

1. Lack of money to invest. People don't have surplus money to risk on a business venture.
2. It's risky. Entrepreneurship means you have to leave your job. Everyone has got certain fixed living expenses to be met, and giving up today's fixed income for an uncertain income in the future is not easy.

3. Lack of mentorship and support systems. People don't have access to mentors who can support in the setting up of a successful enterprise.
4. Lack of knowledge and experience.

Any business model that addresses these four concerns will be a catalyst for an entrepreneurship boom in the country. Any such solution can be a ray of light for millions of people who really want to take up entrepreneurship, but are unable to do so due to one or more of the reasons listed above.

I propose building a direct selling business can be a viable solution and can serve as a zero-risk training ground for future entrepreneurs. Here are some factors that make direct selling a perfect entrepreneurship training school:

1. Robust training and development system with mentors for daily field support. Every good direct selling company and team have an evolved system of training and development that gradually trains you through classroom and field training on all aspects of entrepreneurship.
2. Starting a direct selling business is virtually free. You just need to do some shopping, and you don't need any office, employees, stock, working capital, set-up, etc. Moreover, there are no fixed working hours and nobody to report to. The company does all this for you. Zero starting cost and zero set-up cost means zero financial risk.
3. The model is designed in such a way that anyone without any specific knowledge and experience can begin. In fact, everyone starts a direct selling business from zero. Step-by-step training and constant support from seniors enables everyone to take off. Learning and earning go hand-in-hand in direct selling.

Honestly speaking, it's a dream come true for anyone who seriously wants real-life entrepreneurship training. Learn everything it takes to be an entrepreneur—people management, building and managing teams, time management, financial management, leadership, sales, public speaking, communication skills, and more—without any of the financial, or other, risks and tensions involved in a typical entrepreneurship venture. Zero investment and zero set-up cost make it easy for anyone to start this business. Direct selling is a wonderful, zero-risk training academy to prepare you for an entrepreneur's life.

We often are in favour of quality network-marketing organizations because the good ones offer sound business-skills training without much cost. These organizations also let you test and hone your interpersonal and intrapersonal intelligence—two of the most important keys.

–Donald Trump & Robert Kiyosaki

With direct selling, it is so easy to test yourself to see if you are made for entrepreneurship and entrepreneurship is made for you. If it works out for you, go ahead and continue it. Even if it doesn't, I am sure you will come out with rich experience that will propel you further in your career.

I meet hundreds of people in my live events who want to leave their job and work full-time on their dream entrepreneurship venture but don't have enough cash reserves to take that bold decision. My advice to them is to start building a direct selling business and save all the income from this source in a fund. Since they are already managing their expenses with their current salary or income, the extra income from direct selling can straightaway be deposited in a separate bank account to create a cash reserve. Plus, building a direct selling business will build the necessary skill-set required for entrepreneurship.

So what are you waiting for? Start direct selling. Build your cash reserve. Learn the skills, and whenever you feel the time is right for you, just take a plunge and be an entrepreneur in the area of your choice. Direct selling is a wonderful, one-of-its-kind training school for entrepreneurship and can be a steppingstone to your entrepreneurial dreams.

Entrepreneurship is living a few years of your life like most people won't, so that you can spend the rest of your life like most people can't.

–Unknown

23

Spiritually Uplifting

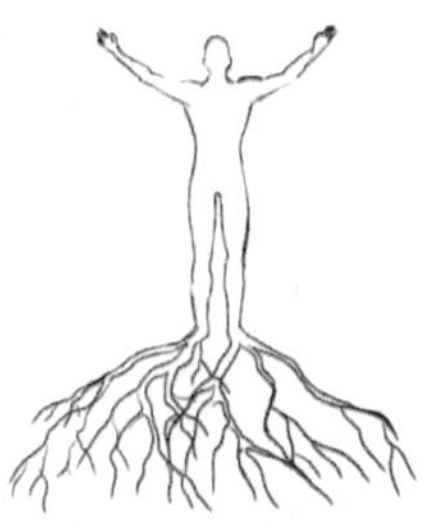

Life is growth. If we stop growing, technically and spiritually, we are as good as dead.

–Morihei Ueshiba

Yes, we all seek money and recognition from our work, but if we can find a way wherein our work can enable us to contribute to the well-being of others in meaningful ways, that would actually be a dream life. Aspiring for more is wonderful. Striving to grow and fulfil dreams is commendable. But what if you can impact other lives while you become rich. Direct selling enables you to do exactly that and these are the reasons why:

1. To the best of my knowledge, direct selling is one of the most democratic ways to become rich. In this business model, you just cannot become rich without helping many others to also become rich. In all other models, there is one business owner and a few other, close people who become rich. But here, for every rich person, there are hundreds of others whose dreams have been fulfilled and who have grown financially along with the main person.
2. In the traditional model, no business owner would share the secrets behind their success. But in direct selling, sharing business

secrets is mandatory because the more you share, the richer you get.

3. In the typical business world, no one helps others in becoming successful. Helping other people to become successful is essential in direct selling.
4. However much they may wish it, a successful business owner will not be able to make others enjoy the same level of success as themselves, because they will not have that kind of money, knowledge and competency. But in direct selling, you don't need any of these. This business gives you a chance to teach people what you know and empower them to become as successful as you.

Once you work with the right company and the right leaders, you will realize it's a business with heart, compassion and deep caring for people.

Many spiritual principles that are considered essential to live a good life are practised in direct selling on a daily basis and form the core working philosophy of this business.

The corporate world operates on the classic principle of survival of the fittest. Anyone who does not perform or takes too much time in understanding things is generally rejected by the institution. What people need are training and help, but what they actually get are admonitions and warnings. The heat is worse in the sales department. It's all work and no heart in most workplaces.

On the other hand, direct selling works purely on the basis of encouraging people to be their best. It rewards progress. People here allow you to learn, understand and experiment at your own pace. Make any number of mistakes and your uplines will still stand by you. If you opt out of the business for a few months, then want to restart, your seniors and the system will welcome you again with open arms. Just as you put in efforts, your seniors and the system also put in efforts for you. It's a business model infused with a tremendous amount of care, encouragement and upliftment. People don't merely dictate what to do; they come along and do the same things with you. In a job, people often pull each other down and are even forced to do things that are unethical, whereas, here, bad performers are not rejected or thrown out; instead, they are given extra care.

Even the choice of words used and body language seen in direct selling is entirely different from that in the corporate world; it's much more uplifting, encouraging and supporting. The culture and the vibes in meetings also differ. The direct selling culture supports human values and offers equal opportunity for all.

We rise by lifting others.

–Robert Ingersoll

Swami Vivekananda said that an atheist is not one who doesn't believe in God but one who doesn't believe in oneself. It is fear that keeps people from believing in themselves. Why so many can't do what they love to do and stay stuck in jobs or professions they hate is because they are afraid. There is only one solution to fear—and that is faith. When faith in the universal power increases, fear vanishes.

Direct selling prepares you to be fearless. Based on my personal experience, I must say that you gradually build absolute faith in yourself and in the universal power as you build your career in direct selling. You face failures repeatedly, you get so many rejections and you hear so many negative comments. You are able to ascertain who your real friends are. People who claimed they would stand with you for the rest of your life go into hiding and stop taking your calls when you ask them to do some shopping or become your business partners.

You will be put to test. Your relationships will be put to test. And remember, anything that doesn't break you makes you stronger. With every rejection and setback, you will grow stronger, until you become fearless. At that stage, you find yourself, and God. Personally speaking, direct selling has been my connection to that supreme power I call God. I have seen that core spiritual values, such as unity, helping others, serving people, relationships, patience, not thinking badly of others, and so on, are taught and practised in plenty in this business.

I also call it the entrepreneurial spirit. Once you have identified this spirit, whatever you do in life will be different. The quality of your work will be entirely renewed. You will feel comfortable with uncertainty. It's about changing your value system, even your DNA itself! Done the right way, a direct selling business can be a really and truly spiritually uplifting experience. It was like that for me and for many others I know, and I wish the same for you.

I would like to offer you one more perspective on work. Whatever you are doing, you must be at one of these three stages of life:

1. Life of survival
    - ✓ You are working hard, and with whatever you earn, you are just about able to manage your expenses and somehow keep it going. You have to compromise on some things and you are worried about the future.
2. Life of success
    - ✓ You are successful at what you are doing and you are among the top 1 per cent of people in your profession in terms of money and reputation. What you have achieved today is the dream position for everyone in your profession or industry.
3. Life of significance
    - ✓ This is a position where not only are you doing very well for yourself but you are also significantly contributing to the well-being of others. You evaluate your life based on the number of people who are better off thanks to you. You measure your success through your contribution. This is the ultimate kind of success and it is attained when your work is aligned with the highest spiritual purpose and practices.

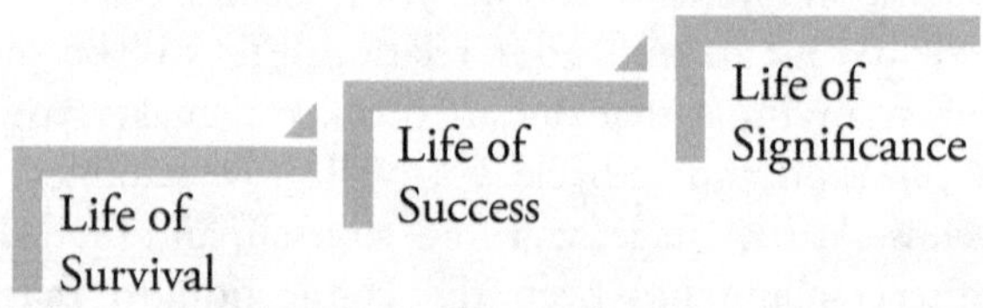

The three stages of life

Direct selling gives every individual an opportunity to live a life of significance. It allows you to build your business and life on the principle of contribution to others. To me, that is incredible, and I will always be indebted to direct selling for blessing me with an ever-expanding opportunity to be a change agent and a source of happiness and prosperity to millions of people.

The deepest of all human needs is the need for meaning and purpose in life and in work.

–Brian Tracy

24
Early Retirement

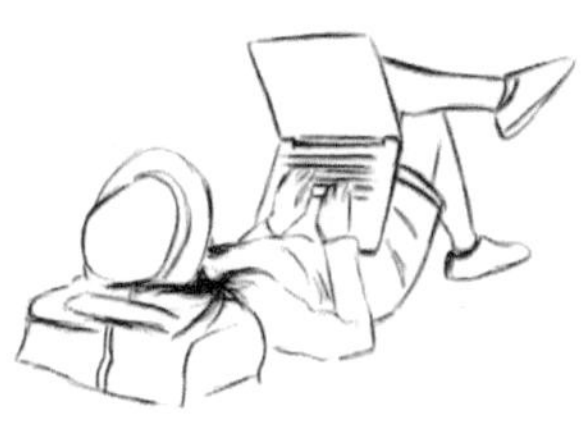

My goal is to build a life I don't need a vacation from.

–Rob Hill

I don't know about you, but in my family, retirement was always considered a day of celebration. Every employee looked forward to the day when they no longer needed to work. All friends and relatives got together for a special retirement party. It was believed that all life long, a person worked hard for this one day when they reached age sixty and didn't have to work anymore. On the flip side, it could also be seen as a situation where they were not competent enough to perform their duties anymore and hence were asked to leave.

As per my understanding, there are two things inherent in this concept of retirement:

1. Your work is a punishment, and you undergo that punishment for thirty to forty glorious years of life in the hope that you will get liberation one day. Then you will be free to do whatever you want to do and truly enjoy life.
2. You will save enough during your working years, so that after retirement, you will continue to get some fixed income to maintain your lifestyle even without working.

I don't want to pass any judgement on this life plan. If you like it and it fits in with your life goals, please go ahead with it. But I would like to propose an early retirement option as follows:

1. If you don't like your work and your work feels like punishment, why do you still want to do it for thirty to forty years of life? Why can't you find an alternative wherein you work for three to five, maybe ten years, after which you have your entire life in front of you to do whatever you always wanted to do. Why wait till sixty to live your dream life?
2. Who said retirement age has to be fifty-eight or sixty? What you need is not an age but a financial set-up for retirement. When the goal is to earn enough during working years, so that we can survive our post-retirement years, why not work on a business model that offers two benefits:
    a. You earn much more than your current expenses so that you can create a reserve for the future.
    b. Build a passive income stream in a few years' time, such that it continues to give you an income, year after year, even without your active involvement.
3. Why retire at all? Why can't we design our life in such a way that we don't need to retire from it. If you can find out what you love most and figure out a way to make money from it, your work becomes fun. The more you work, the more fun you have, and the bigger is the amount of money you make. The key is to design every single day of your life in such a way that you look forward to your destination even as you enjoy the journey. Imagine how wonderful it would be if the journey itself became the destination!

I urge you to find ways and means of saving many years of your life and retiring early, if at all you intend to retire. Don't wait for thirty to forty years to get something that can be attained in five to ten years. I really invite you to create a life where you will decide how much you are worth. You will decide your work timings and whom you want to work with. You will determine your increments and you will write your own pay checks.

There are countless ways of achieving this and I know hundreds of people who have done it in many different ways. If you can't find something that enables you to do that, try direct selling. It has given me and thousands of others the early retirement we were looking for. I don't know how you have viewed direct selling until now, but approach it afresh with the perspective of early retirement and explore for yourself whether it fits into your scheme of things.

Retirement is not the end of work. It is the end of mandatory work.

–Unknown

25

Build a Business that the Family Can Run Together

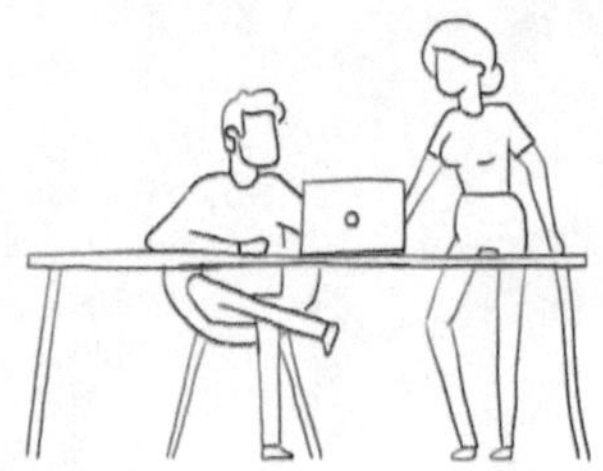

A man should never neglect his family for business.

–Walt Disney

We spend a majority of our waking hours at work. Nowadays, in most households, both partners are working and every morning, both set off in two different directions for work. Each has their own set of work situations and challenges. They come back exhausted and prepare for the next day. Those running businesses face their own set of challenges.

You must have seen married couples at restaurants who just sit there in silence because they have nothing to discuss. Or else, each of them has so much to say about their individual work that they are not interested in listening to what the other has to say. I know many couples who don't have anything in common to talk about, and all their lives, they struggle to achieve a work-life balance.

Imagine building a business together with your partner. Imagine being together with your partner the whole day. Talking, eating, laughing and travelling together, facing challenges, finding solutions and building your future together. You won't even realize where work ends and fun begins or where fun ends and work begins!

When you build a business together, you build your life and

a great relationship together. You handle the ups and downs of life together. You see different facets of the other person and you learn how you both can complement and support each other in different situations. Even this joy of changing the financial future of your family together is a big reward.

I have held a corporate job for 4 years and have been a serial entrepreneur for more than 12 years now. I have trained and coached more than 7,00,000 people in the past 16 years, and with my experience, I can firmly say that direct selling is undoubtedly one of the best options available if you intend to build a business with your family. Theoretically, any business can be developed by a family together, but in the traditional businesses, there are certain specific capabilities and requirements that both partners may not have. Once you read the 12 reasons I list below, you may realize why I believe direct selling can easily and practically be developed as a family business.

Direct selling is truly a family business for many reasons such as these:

1. In spite of holding different full-time jobs, any couple can choose to build this business together part-time.
2. You decide your working hours.
3. No formal degree or specific experience is required for starting this business, so anybody in the family can join anytime.
4. You don't need any infrastructure or legal work to be done before your family can join you in the business.
5. People of any age and gender can do it.
6. Most direct selling companies support and recognize families who are building the business together.
7. When a couple is building the business together, whenever required, either one can handle the business while the other can take care of the children and home.
8. Most of the training programmes allow children to attend the events.
9. The business generally offers many trips and travel opportunities wherein families can travel together.
10. Children learn the value of passive income and financial freedom at an early age.

11. Since most of our life goals are family goals, when a family works together on those goals, it's a rewarding experience and success comes faster.
12. The very core principles of the direct selling business also promote family togetherness.

Sticking with your family is what makes it a family.

–Mitch Albom

I can say from experience that the best of friendships and companionships get strengthened when you face a crisis together. When you and your partner go through challenges together, it strengthens your bond. You get to know each other better and grow emotionally intelligent together. You respect each other better, mature together, and see each other much more closely in different situations. You learn to understand each other as an individual and understand why you both do what you do. This is incredible and invaluable for the development of the relationship. Your relationship with your husband/wife should go to the next level when you build a direct selling business together.

These memories of building a legacy together will stay with you for the rest of life. Ordinarily, people take holidays to spend time together, but in direct selling, you and your partner will travel the world together to build the business. Every day, you are on a holiday. I know people who found their partners while building this business. I know couples whose relationships really improved after coming to this business.

My wife and I resigned our jobs in 2007 to build this business. For the first few years, we had some awesome days and some really rough patches. We built new teams and visited new cities. Twice, my key teams quit and we had to rebuild the business right from scratch. There was even a period where we had no business and no income. The conversations that we had on those dark nights gave such strength and endurance to our relationship that it seems as if we are falling in love with each other more with every passing day.

My wife and I travel to events together. Many people harbour this myth that business and family are two different things. When people see us together as a happy couple joyfully building their future together, they are not only inspired to make a good financial future but also to develop quality relationships. I could make it so far thanks to my wife being with me at every moment through the journey.

What a joy it is to build a business with your family, and not just for your family. Yes, there may be moments of arguments and conflicts, but that happens in every family. Moreover, from personal experience, I can tell you this: If you are in the direct selling business, you will forget and forgive faster because there are people looking up to you and you may have to go on stage together that evening.

Right from childhood, my brother Gaurav and I wanted to stay together. But I was in a sales and marketing job in Chandigarh and he was a software consultant in Gurgaon. In four years I had changed three locations, and he was relocating to USA for his work. When this business opportunity came along, we both took it up, and within a few months, we both resigned our jobs. Now we are staying together in a joint family for more than a decade. Life is awesome. There are ten of us in the same villa along with our staff. The joy, laughter and peace of mind in my home round the clock is priceless and has been possible only because of direct selling.

So if you are someone like me who always wants his family to be with him, just explore direct selling. You may find the solutions you have been looking for all your life.

Coming together is a beginning; keeping together is progress; working together is success.

–Edward Everett Hale

26
Excellent Part-Time Business Opportunity

Don't wait to be an entrepreneur before you start. Just begin and you will become an entrepreneur in the process of pursuing your vision.

–Deepak Bajaj

I am a die-hard fan of entrepreneurship, not because an entrepreneur owns a business, but more so for the qualities of an entrepreneur—free, risk-taker, accountable, responsible, result-driven and passionate. I strongly believe each one of these virtues is essential to be able to live a life of passion, abundance and meaningful contribution. Entrepreneurship is about having a vision, taking responsibility and striving for more.

I strongly urge you—even if you never start a business of your own, be enterprising and develop the virtues that come with it. It's a great business school that will provide lifelong education. Which is why, I love to promote anything that builds entrepreneurial virtues in people and makes it easier for them to get a taste of entrepreneurship.

Even corporates want employees to have these characteristics. Look at the typical qualities of an entrepreneur—accountability, creativity, emotional resilience, solution-oriented thinking, commitment to results, ability to handle failures, and willingness to work more than what is dictated by the clock. Which corporate doesn't need people with these traits?

I can foresee the emergence of a novel concept I call 'entreployees'. A new culture is on the anvil where companies will work with people who are part-entrepreneurs and part-employees. In this new system, there will be some conditions, performance parameters, tasks and results to be delivered, of course. Yet, at the same time, autonomy and entrepreneurial freedom will be given to the person performing those tasks in a way that is beneficial to both the organization and the employee.

I can envision this new model taking shape in just a few years. So even if you don't want to start your own venture, I invite everyone to join this new tribe of entreployees, and I think direct selling can be a perfect training ground for this.

Being an entrepreneur isn't just a job title, and it isn't just about starting a company. It's a state of mind. It's about seeing connections others can't, seizing opportunities others won't, and forging new directions that others haven't.

–Tory Burch

Why are many people scared of entrepreneurship? The biggest reason is the risk factor involved. You invest, make a set-up, and then start marketing. But you start earning only after you sell. If sales don't pick up, your initial fixed cost and monthly variable costs pile up as losses.

A part-time entrepreneurship opportunity is a dream come true for millions. On top of it, if that opportunity doesn't ask for any big initial investment and fixed set-up, it's a jackpot. Direct selling is definitely one such opportunity. You don't need any big investment, office, staff, or set-up to begin. You decide your working hours. There is a training and development system that equips you with all the required knowledge, skills and techniques. Your seniors and the system will give you all the necessary ground support everyday on your successful entrepreneurial journey.

On a side note, personally, I don't believe in the concept of part-time involvement. I have used this term here only to signify that you can do direct selling alongside your current job or profession. So, even though your hours may be fewer, you must give your 100 per cent in those hours to make this business venture successful.

Consider the owners of Reliance or Tata or Mahindra who run several businesses together. Can you tell which business is part-time and which is full-time? It's all about time management and stretching yourself to meet the bigger goals. So if you couldn't get on the entrepreneurship bandwagon because of the risk involved, you don't have the same excuse in case of direct selling.

A word of caution. This part-time entrepreneurship with zero risk and no set-up cost may bring in a casual attitude or outlook. Sometimes, your investment determines your seriousness. Since you have not made any investment and it's only some shopping, you don't take it seriously as you would in case of a business. No fixed timings sometimes becomes no time available. Plus, your salary is covering your current expenses anyways, so why work hard for some extra income? No boss and no place to report to turns too soon into a holiday.

If you can handle these aspects with discipline, you are on your way to your dream life with direct selling.

In the world of entrepreneurs, you don't need a college education. You need a proper education.

–Robert T. Kiyosaki

27

Learn the Art of Developing Relationships that Empower

Business, after all, is nothing more than a bunch of human relationships.

–Lee Iacocca

The more you progress in life, the more you realize that all growth happens by way of growing relationships. Relationships are the backbone of any organization, be it a home or a corporation. Hence, developing relationships is definitely a skill worth developing in life. But, as with any other skill, if you need to develop this skill of building and nurturing relationships, you need to change yourself too, and change is not easy.

You will change only for either of these two reasons:

1. Change is highly rewarding and you value there ward that is coming with this change.

2. Change is the only option you have.

Direct selling encourages and empowers you to change yourself to develop this beautiful skill of developing relationships. People are your only resource in this industry, and if you want to grow and prosper, your team must perform well. Your team will perform well only when they follow you and work according to the pre-defined success system. All this is possible only if you have a fairly good relationship with your people. You know how tough it can be to get work done from people who are reporting to you. But here, you are asking people to work without any authority over them! This is possible only by way of your relationship and influence with them.

It is important to remember that people will stay in your organization not because of any formal authority exerted over them, but because of your relationship with them. You will learn this skill indirect selling, but it will help you everywhere. Howsoever logical people may be, opportunities are definitely passed on only to those with whom we share good relationships. After all, every organization is nothing but a set of people, and people move with relationships. Even at home you need quality relationships with your spouse, parents and children. As you ascend levels at the workplace, your job is to delegate and get work done by others, and this can be easily achieved when you develop good relationships.

If you believe business is built on relationships, make building them your business.

–Scott Stratten

I want you to go to the next level while developing relationships. You should master the art of developing relationships that are empowering, ones that give you energy and strength, that inspire you to be your best and propel you to a higher level. Hone the ability to identify those relationships that drain you of your energy and find smart ways to minimize your involvement in such relationships. This clarity will save you time and energy. Please note that I am not advising you to only take from relationships. Be a contributor. Be a giver. But be among people who appreciate you, encourage you and pull you up. Once you find such people, develop good, empowering, win-win relationships with them.

The size of your achievements will be directly proportional to the number of empowering relationships you develop. Master this invaluable skill and enhance your quality of life.

Developing a relationship with someone you admire, who can encourage you to reach your full potential, is something that everyone can benefit from.

–Mandy Moore

28

Earn While You Learn

Learning is a treasure that will follow its owners everywhere.

–Chinese proverb

In every business, there is a gestation period—the time taken for a new business to start showing results. This period ranges from a few months to a few years, depending on the type of business. Every business owner is mentally prepared to undertake losses for the first few months up to a few years in anticipation of future profits. The gestation period is the toughest period for an entrepreneur because expenses are always greater than the income and the business owner manages the expenses from their cash reserve.

Some businesses close down in the gestation period itself, while many others close operations over the next five years. Every such closure means huge financial losses for the owner. This period is also called the learning period, and in a traditional business, earning will start only after you have completed a few months or years in this learning period. This scares many people and prevents them from taking the risk of starting a business.

Direct selling is an amazing business model with low or zero gestation period. First, register with a direct selling company.

Understand the basics and start your meetings the very same day. No waiting time. Sell some products, get some associates, and you can start earning right away. It's a dream come true where you can earn while you learn. Earning and learning occur simultaneously.

Since you don't have any set-up cost nor any cost of running the business, all the income you earn is your profit. This is one of the most profitable businesses with virtually infinite return on investment (ROI). All you need is a dream, willingness to learn and commitment to work regularly.

Earn while you learn is one more feature of direct selling that is basically democratizing entrepreneurship, making it much easier for a common person to venture into it.

The capacity to learn is a gift; the ability to learn is a skill; the willingness to learn is a choice.

–Brian Herbert

29
Be a Champion of Public Speaking

There are lives made out of speeches and there are speeches made out of life.

–Ra

Public speaking is one of the most powerful tools God has given to human beings to influence and transform others. The biggest of revolutions, wars and definitive changes in the world were initiated and sustained through the power of speech. There is power of life and death in your tongue. Words are the most powerful drug on earth. Words are so powerful that it is said that wounds caused by a sword can heal, but those caused by words can never heal. Just think about the power that allowed Mahatma Gandhi, Adolf Hitler and Vladimir Lenin, to name a few giants, to lead some of the biggest revolutions in the history of the world. What empowered these leaders to influence millions of people to blindly follow them? It was their effective public speaking skills.

Whatever you may be doing in your life, irrespective of your job, profession, age, gender, location or educational background, I highly recommend you master this one skill—public speaking. Every hour invested in developing this all-important skill will take you years ahead in your career and in life. We all aspire to achieve positions of leadership and influence, but there can be no leadership and influence without mastery in public speaking.

Please don't be under this false illusion that public speaking skills are required only when you are a speaker or leader. You need good public speaking abilities on countless occasions in everyday life too. For example, when you deal with a group of five to ten people in any situation—when dealing with your team, or your residential society, or any association you are a member of, or with your colleagues in a formal meeting, or at a school function for your kids, or when faced with any opportunity to share your views among people. Good public speaking skills will uplift your image in front of people and enhance your influence.

I was born in a small village of a few hundred homes. My parents were government employees and so were all my relatives. I studied in government-run Hindi medium schools and by the time I graduated from Class 12, I had already changed 6 schools. Then I tried out different career options and simply did what felt right at that moment. After juggling to be a doctor, CA, bank employee or corporate manager, today I am a serial entrepreneur, a #1 bestselling author with my books translated in 6 languages, with videos watched by more than 3 million people every month in more than 100 countries. I have already trained and coached more than 7,00,000 people. I am featured in several magazines, including on the cover of a prestigious magazine. I received the Best Debut Author 2018 award. My training workshops run houseful and are known to bring about instant change and lasting transformation.

Yes, I worked hard on my total personal transformation, but if you ask me about that one key skill that was most instrumental in my success and growth—it is public speaking and communication skills. I am still working on these and want to influence a billion lives in the next couple of years. In my workshops, I teach my participants everything this journey has taught me and all the tools that brought about this massive personal transformation in my own life. But if I have the choice of insisting on your developing one key skill for life, I would repeatedly say choose to build your public speaking skills.

Go for it. I insist you devote at least an hour every week to hone this skill. I know you will forever be grateful to me for this recommendation. Most participants in my Public Speaking and Communication Skills workshop have reported deeply significant changes in their lives after developing this skill.

The worst speech you will ever give will be far better than the one you never give.

–Fred E. Miller

Like any other skill, public speaking, too, is entirely acquirable. Tap into all the basic knowledge and tools available, and find more and more opportunities to practise the same. Video record your speeches, review them, and keep making corrections. You will grow better and more confident with every speech. But one thing is for sure—public speaking is one skill that requires constant practice. So any amount of knowledge is not enough if you cannot make speeches on a consistent basis.

In my workshop, we make our participants repeatedly practise and internalize key components of excellent public speaking. Let me give you an overview here:

1. Content
2. Rehearsals
3. Mindset
4. Stories and life experiences
5. Intention
6. Stage management tools
7. Emotional management tools

Never underestimate the power of your speech. 99 per cent of people fail to get any results in public speaking because they are focused on just delivering a talk. Delivery, dress, technique, content—all these are definitely important. But please remember, the objective of delivering any speech is transformation and change. If the speech does everything else without getting this result, to me that speech is a miserable failure. If you prepare your speech around these seven essential components, you will never fail to bring about the desired results and complete transformation for your audience.

Direct selling offers one such platform that will give you unlimited opportunities for public speaking. The very best speakers and trainers on earth never get as many speaking opportunities as a successful network marketer gets. Not only do you get opportunities to speak, but you also get to see the results of your speech in your sales volumes. Above all, what direct selling offers is a conducive and supportive environment that inspires, encourages, trains and supports you to fine-tune your skill.

I hope I can see you live someday, as you deliver your speech. Go for it.

Make sure you have finished speaking before you audience has finished listening.

–Dorothy Sarnoff

30

Use It to Fuel Your Passion

Your work is going to fill a large part of your life, and the only way to be truly satisfied is to do what you believe is great work. And the only way to do great work is to love what you do. If you haven't found it yet, keep looking, and don't settle. As with all matters of the heart, you will know when you find it.

–Steve Jobs

Deep within, each one of us has a calling. Some call it purpose, some call it passion, and some others call it life mission. Whatever word we use for it, there is something that each one of us really and truly wants to do. While growing up, every one of us had our own favourite superhero, and every time someone asked us—'What do you want to become in life?'—we had a spark in our eyes and we knew what we wanted to become. Sometimes we said it out loud, and at other times, we chose to keep it to ourselves. But each one of us had a deep desire to be someone special. I am yet to meet someone who doesn't want to play big with their life, who doesn't aspire to achieve the next level of greatness. Each one of us craves to do more, to be more, and to do our own thing. But the irony is that most of us explore everything else in life except that one thing where our heart is. And it at all any of us do it, it just ends up being a hobby.

What a tragedy it is to see someone whose heart is in playing the guitar, but is performing surgeries in operation theatres, day after day. Or, someone who wants to be a playback singer but has been toiling at construction sites as a civil engineer for decades instead. Or, someone who feels alive when teaching kids, but is forced to be a CA, crunching dead numbers all day. I have seen managers during my corporate job days who actually wanted to be singers, YouTubers, creative designers or musicians, but were instead fighting to sell more and more motorcycles, month after month. We humans are the most beautiful and smartest creation of God. We have reached the moon and Mars. We have conquered mountains and oceans. Yet, why can't we find ways and means of doing what we are truly passionate about doing?

Why are we punishing ourselves day after day? And then we keep wondering why we are not happy. Most people are doing whatever it is they are doing not out of any passion, but just to make a livelihood. Basically, they do it for the paycheck. If you doubt this, try to figure out how many people will still come to work if there is no salary. It's as if people have given themselves punishment. In early years, teachers imposed it, at times parents or some relatives did it, and in many cases, later in life, people choose this themselves. Have you ever come across someone who is undergoing punishment and is happy and joyful? I don't think so.

When I was 5 years old, my mother always told me that happiness was the key to life. When I went to school, they asked me what I wanted to be when I grew up. I wrote down 'happy'. They told me I didn't understand the assignment, and I told them they didn't understand life.

–John Lennon

Why do you think his happens? There is only one reason—money. We were indoctrinated into believing that our passion will not bring in money. That passion is awesome but it cannot fill our stomach. First and foremost, make yourself employable, and once settled in life, you can do whatever you want. Every time we tried to venture outside the text books or established norms, we were ridiculed and punished. I am not making a judgement on whether that was right or wrong.

I am proposing that if the whole point is money, then why suffer without money in the wrong job or profession for your whole life. Why don't you work on something for just a few years and solve your money problem? As it is, you are doing what you don't like, so it won't matter if you like the new work or not. But instead of punishing yourself all life long and still being broke, why not punish yourself for a few years by doing something that gives you more money and a system that will continue to give you a regular income, month on month. Once your basic monetary requirement is fulfilled, you are free to pursue what you have always wanted to.

Please think about it. You are doing something you don't like and that is keeping you unhappy. You thought you would get more money by doing it, but most of you don't seem to have more money than before and are living paycheck to paycheck, in spite for working for so many years. Don't you think you have been fooled into buying into a theory that is wrong? But it's never too late to do what is right. So the simple solution is to build a source of income that will continue to give you enough money to manage your expenses. Once that is achieved in the next few years, you can pursue your passion.

There is no passion to be found playing small—in settling for a life that is less than the one you are capable of living.

–Nelson Mandela

But my job doesn't end with only giving you ideas; I am here to provide solutions. If you are really looking for an opportunity that can be established in a few years in such a way that it will cover your expenses, gives you some bank balance for contingency, and also a constant source of income, then I ask you to explore a direct selling business.

Please know that I am not asking you to get into direct selling just for the heck of it. I am proposing you do it for that sum of money you need to be able to get out of that punishing job or profession you are currently stuck in. Do it even if you don't like it. Liking should not be a concern anyway because whatever you are doing right now is also not to your liking.

So build your direct selling business as per your schedule. Build it with the right foundation and system. Once it is established, manage it with your team system and start pursuing whatever is your passion.

One more piece of advice. Whatever you are doing right now,

please do it with 100 per cent heart and soul. Joyfully do whatever you are doing while constantly keeping an eye out for solutions and better opportunities. In the years when I worked at my day job, I too was one of the most high-performing employees. I was one of the youngest people to hold the position of area manager in my company. Everyday I did more than what was expected from me in my role, but I kept looking out for something that would allow me to pursue my passion.

I had an unpredictable career. I set out to be a doctor, then changed my mind to become a CA, but finally ended up doing an MBA. I got into a corporate job, then resigned at the peak of my career to be an entrepreneur. Along with my businesses, now I am a bestselling author, speaker, trainer, coach and social media influencer. In hindsight, I can say that this was my childhood calling. But I kept building my life by doing to the best of my ability whatever came my way. I improved myself month on month through books and training programmes. I saved while I earned and strengthened my finances year after year. I think the magic key to life is to go as far as you can see, and once you reach one destination, God will show you the next one.

If you can't stop thinking about it, don't stop working on it.

–Michael Jordan

31
Open Opportunity Where Everyone is Welcome

Life opens up opportunities to you, and you either take them or you stay afraid of taking them.

–Jim Carrey

Life usually presents opportunities with some conditions attached. Every profession entails certain specific skills, qualities and qualifications; thus, every job advertisement comes with specific requirements. Setting up a business too has its own set of requirements. Educational and experiential background, including the school and college you attended, your academic records, the cities you have lived in—all of these factors can haunt you for decades. People will form opinions about you based on your educational degrees, financial background, places of study, the city you live in, and so on and so forth.

So, in the corporate world, if you are an engineer with a degree that is not from an IIT or any other equally prestigious college, you will be treated differently for the rest of your life. Likewise, if you have done your MBA at any institution other than the IIMs or the other top B-Schools, people may question your credentials. You may have made great strides in life, but these name tags will keep chasing you.

In this scenario, it is so heartening to find an opportunity that is truly an equal opportunity for all. Whatever your age, educational or financial background, gender, city, school, language, etc., you can build a successful direct selling business. You get all the facilities and support that are available to everyone else. In fact, nobody ever asks you about any of these things, because nobody is concerned about them. You are accepted with an open heart and open arms. It's such an incredible free enterprise system where nobody asks questions about your past, where everybody accepts you as you are. It's a wonderful community of simple people working together to fulfil their dreams. The model has been designed in such a way that each one supports the other, and everyone moves forward together.

I believe the biggest kind of respect you can give a human being is to accept them just as they are without any judgement or prejudice. And over a period of time, this has become part of the DNA of direct sellers. I really admire this industry for its core human values—compassion, non-judgemental outlook, service, unconditional support, adding value to people, putting others first, equality and transparency, among others.

The direct selling culture is so much more empowering and encouraging than that prevalent in the corporate world. Just imagine the contrast: Here, instead of saying, 'If you don't perform, you will lose your job', people say, 'Let me help you do better.' People here are ready to give you as much time as you need to learn. They are always by your side, willing to teach you and support you. Here, you get what I call the license to make mistakes. In this business, you are encouraged to learn by making mistakes, correcting them and getting smarter by the day.

The direct selling stage will never reward you nor give you any extra privileges for what you have done prior to starting this business. All your past achievements and failures are immaterial. The only thing that matters and that will be recognized is what you achieve once you have started direct selling.

If any of you have been adversely affected by your past, and feel that something from your past has been preventing you from making progress in life, welcome to the world of direct selling where everyone is welcome.

You can't go back and change the beginning, but you can start where you are and change the ending.

–C.S. Lewis

The direct selling model is so simple, flexible and transparent that anyone can adopt it and excel in it.

For employees, this is an excellent second income source that can be developed without any major investment and set-up.

Students can take up this business as a part-time job and learn so many invaluable skills. They usually have more free time, which they can utilize to learn and earn and make an excellent career for themselves.

Professionals anyway work independently. They can easily build an extra income source in their spare time at their own convenience.

It's an excellent diversification opportunity for business owners, who, without any fixed investment and specialized knowledge, can start one more line of business.

It's an excellent opportunity for housewives and women who want to work from home. While they manage their families, they can spare a few hours whenever convenient to build this business.

Retired people can also take up this business as per their convenience and earn an assured stream of income.

Luck is what happens when preparation meets opportunity.

–Seneca

Anyone who likes the working philosophy and values of direct selling is welcome to start and be a part of this industry. Yes, the seniors and the training system will give recommendations for building the business in the right way, but these are only suggestions. You have the ultimate authority to decide how you would like to build your business. After all, it's entirely your business.

Direct selling asks only three simple things of a person:

1. You have dreams. You want to change some things for yourself and your family.
2. You are willing to learn the principles of success in this business.

3. You are ready to take complete ownership of your business and will give your best efforts to build your business.

So leave the past behind, focus on your dreams, and give it a shot.

What lies behind you and what lies in front pales in comparison to what lies inside you.

–Ralph Waldo Emerson

It's Not About the Business—It's About You

I am always surprised that people treat direct selling as everything but a business. Please understand that it's not a get-rich-quick scheme, or a lottery, or a hobby; it is a business like any other. It waives off conditions such as investment, showroom, staff, stock or working capital, but it still needs everything else that is required for success just as in any other venture. It will need hard work, commitment, perseverance, skills and adherence to the principles of entrepreneurship.

I remember an incident that occurred in 2009, following my seminar in Ludhiana, Punjab. After the event, a distributor introduced me to his so-called high-profile guest. He said, 'My name is Joginder Singh (name changed to respect privacy) and we are in the bicycle spare parts business.' I said, 'My name is Deepak Bajaj and I am in the direct selling business.' He replied, 'That's ok, but what do you do?' So I repeated, 'I do direct selling. The same thing that you have been listening to, for the past two hours.' He insisted, 'That's ok, but what is your main work?' Even after thirty minutes of persuasion, I failed to convince this gentleman that direct selling was my full-time profession!

I am surprised that when it comes to any other entrepreneurship venture, people are absolutely fine with investing money and time for a few years before they can start earning profits. In fact, even if it takes two to five years before you can start earning profits, it is considered good. But when it comes to network marketing, people start expecting profits after three meetings, or after one week in the business. When that doesn't happen, they start blaming the business and quit. Please remember, if you treat something like a business and behave as any business owner would, you will get returns just as you would in any other business. But if you treat it like a hobby, please don't expect returns. Nobody gets paid for enjoying a hobby for an hour or so every week.

If you are not ready to take this business seriously, I honestly suggest you don't take it up. This field of work came into existence long before most of you were born. It has already been flourishing in 179 countries (WFDSA Annual Report 2019) for decades. It's you who needs to prove if you are worthy of it. This business has got everything it takes; now you need to prove if you have everything it takes to make it big and to fulfil your dreams. Know that it's not about the business now; it's about you. Please be aware that your failure in this business is simply your failure and absolutely not the failure of this industry.

If an entrepreneur starts a real estate or financial services or e-commerce business and fails, we wouldn't say that the industry is a failure; we simply conclude that this particular individual couldn't do what was expected to succeed in the business. When we don't link an individual's failure to the whole industry's failure in any other field, then why do that here? This is also a business with its own set of principles and a better training and support system than that found in any other industry on earth. I have never seen this kind of support in any other industry. So, despite that, if someone fails, it's purely and wholly their fault and not at all a mistake or something lacking in the business itself.

I am really surprised when people say that they have lost thousands of rupees in direct selling. How can you lose even one rupee when there is absolutely zero joining fees and all you have done is shopping for some products that you need or want to try? As a matter of fact, people who think they can make fast money simply by joining a direct selling company are the first ones to be cheated. Their greed overpowers their intellect. They know it is not true. Yet they invest huge sums and later blame the industry.

I recommend you read my book, *Be A Network Marketing Millionaire*. It's been on bestseller charts ever since its launch in June

2018 and has consistently been the most read, most followed and most recommended essential guidebook on building a successful, ethical and long-lasting network marketing business. Attend some events, meet some leaders or seniors, get a feel of it, and then start building your commitment. Strictly stay away from companies that charge starting fees or ask you for a big investment.

Another thing. Please choose the company and team wisely. There is a guideline included in this book, and there are several videos on choosing the right company on my YouTube channel as well. My YouTube channel, 'Deepak Bajaj', is considered to be one of the most reliable and biggest resources for learning anything about direct selling. Work with a good team that has a successful track record and a powerful training and development system.

If you decide to do this business, develop it like any other entrepreneurship venture. Enjoy the benefit of earning while learning. Be teachable. Be committed to working as per the system and ethics of the industry. Remember, it is never a wrong time to do what is right.

What lies behind us and what lies ahead of us are tiny matters compared to what lives within us.

–Henry David Thoreau

Many people ask me how much time it takes on an average to be successful in this business. I can't answer this question, because you can take an average of numbers, but not of human beings. Moreover, I don't believe anybody is an average human being. Each one of us is unique—I am unique, you are too. Microsoft, Reliance, Infosys and Facebook—all of them took different amounts of time and all of them became successful entrepreneurs with their own story. You too will write your own story. The key question is not how much time it will take, but what you need to change in yourself, and what you need to become to achieve the next level of success. Trust me, as you continue making those changes in yourself, you will get closer to accomplishing whatever you want to achieve. I have experienced this all my life and I want you to experience the same for yourself.

Never forget—it's a journey. It's a process. It will take time. Be clear about your action plan and just keep moving forward. In fact, real entrepreneurs never ask this question: When will my work be over? Being an entrepreneur is work in progress. Keep learning, doing, making mistakes, growing and evolving, and after a while, growth and contribution become your drivers. Entrepreneurs are problem solvers. I love my life. Even though it has been a decade since I have been financially free for the rest of my life, I am probably working harder now than I did when I started out. Solving problems, becoming better, exploring new dimensions and discovering parts of me that I never knew existed, serving, contributing and giving back to society—all these things drive me and keep me going joyfully on this journey.

It's simple if you want to be in the top 1 per cent. You need to do what the top 1 per cent of people do, and they do exactly what I just told you to do. You choose.In my workshops, I usually ask people—how many people they know who have been working for twenty to thirty years in jobs or in their own businesses, who are financially free now? Almost all of them say they don't know anyone in their circle who has achieved financial abundance or passive income even after twenty to thirty years of work.

If you want to achieve in the next few years what most people cannot achieve in thirty years, be very clear that you are in a different game. The question is: Are you willing to give yourself a chance to play this new game of life?

I have realized that there are no failures in this business, only quitters. If someone has the tenacity to stay in the business and to grow and learn from their mistakes, that person is bound to succeed. But if you quit, it's definitely not about the business; it's about you.

My best friend is the one who brings out the best in me.

–Henry Ford

How to Choose the Right Direct Selling Company

If you want to start your own direct selling business, the next pertinent question is which company you should work with. Selecting the right company is an absolutely essential factor of your success. Many in the direct selling business start working with the first company they come across. If your first company is a good company, you are lucky. If you are already working with a company, or are about to start, please remember that you can build a great business only with a good company.

Every direct seller will tell you this: 'Our company is number one.' Or other things such as, 'Our products are great, our turnover is big, our income plan is awesome, our reward system is great, we are the best company in this business…' and so on. But being a reader of my books, I want to prepare you to make an intelligent and well-informed choice. After all, it's about your life, your dreams and your future. I highly recommend that you invest some time in choosing the right company. I am not advising you to sit on it and drag this decision for days or weeks, but if you have made up your mind and you liked any direct selling presentation, then I strongly suggest that you meet some seniors and attend some upcoming events before you decide to work with any company.

Working with the right direct selling company is one of the pre-requisites of building a stable and growing network marketing business. As far as legality is concerned, every country has its own set of guidelines for direct selling companies; you can check what they are in your country. I am listing here a few basic essentials that you must check on before starting your direct selling business. If any one or more of these basics are missing in any company, I really doubt whether you will be able to build the kind of business I have described in this book. So be very careful in your selection. Here is my basic fourteen-point guideline for choosing the right company:

1. Make sure the company has an excellent track record for the last few years. Find out about the experience and credentials of the management team. Don't be lured into this belief—To make it big, you need to start with a company in its initial stages. That's not true. In fact, most start-ups in any industry close down in the first few years of the business. I recommend you do your own due diligence and be very careful about where you are going to invest your hard work, time and reputation. Several fly-by-night operators cheat innocent people with false claims, so be cautious.

   The management must be visionary and adaptable to new changes. It should perform its duties conscientiously to keep growing. The distributors must work really hard and the company must stay ahead of competition.

2. A good company never charges any joining fees to start the business. Stay away from companies that ask you to buy products for huge amounts.

3. There have to be genuine products or services that offer value for money to their customers. A simple way to check this is to see if the products can be sold even without the business opportunity. Some companies offer dummy products just to bypass government policies.

4. Income must come from genuine sale of products or services. Stay away from companies that offer some fixed returns. The income plan should be transparent and without any hidden conditions.

5. A proven and powerful training and development system for your overall development is absolutely essential for

building a stable and growing business. So many committed people have failed because they didn't get the right mentor and training. A proven system that has already produced achievers is mandatory for success. Moreover, you will be able to build a big and productive team only through a system. One big reason why people come into direct selling is the possibility of earning passive income, and ongoing passive income is possible only with a good training system in place.

People are the biggest resource in any direct selling organization, and I strongly believe that only good people can do good business. So look for an organization where the focus is your overall development and not just short-term sales collection. The training system should not only equip you with mandatory business skills but also help develop your personality, character, and leadership and communication skills. It should fundamentally put you on a growth path.

6. Look for a company with unique and result-oriented products/services. In the direct selling industry, customer recommendation is the only way of building business, and recommendations will happen only if the products are of good quality and deliver results. A wide range of high-quality and easily marketable products is essential for success.
7. The income plan should be easy to understand and explain. You don't know who will become part of your team in the months to come and how they will explain the income and rewards plan. If you cannot explain your income plan in sixty seconds, then it's too complicated. Duplication is key in this business, and anything that is complicated just cannot be duplicated.
8. Does your upline team have a clear action plan for you? Motivation alone is not enough. Before you commit yourself to building this business, you should be very clear about the amount of effort required for you to achieve your goals. If your seniors are not able to give you a clear action plan, I don't consider it a place that is conducive to your stable and growing future.

9. Make sure the company is following all statutory requirements. That all income is given as per tax laws prevalent in the country. Check to ensure the company has a spotless payment record.
10. The company's products should be so good that you would like to use them for yourself and your family. Customers are the best brand ambassadors of a company's products, and sharing good things is basic human nature. When your associates love the products, sharing or promoting the products is easier for them, which ultimately brings consistent business. All good income plans reward repurchase of the products by its distributors.
11. No fixed packages or kits for starting the business. People should choose whatever they want for themselves.
12. Make sure that recruitment is not compulsory for getting income. Income must be generated based on the amount of products sold and not on the number of people recruited.
13. An effective channel for easy and timely availability of products/services to the customers is also essential.
14. Carefully select the right seniors (called uplines). They are the ones who will be meeting your first set of prospects. You are going to follow them and learn from them. Look for good leaders with an excellent track record, positive reputation, stability, excellent achievement, good level of business building skills and good character. They should inspire you and empower you to do more and be more. Their ways of working should match with yours. When you look at seniors, or when you attend an event, does their value system match yours? The language, the culture and what they teach should inspire you and make you proud of what you are doing.

    You will meet many direct sellers who keep changing companies the way people change shirts. If someone switches companies once or twice for valid reasons, it is understandable, but if changing companies has become a habit for someone, please rethink before you trust them with your future. They may not be wrong, but I want you to make a wise judgement.

The above set of guidelines is not a fixed set of rules or laws, but they are essential requirements for your success. These are based purely on my thirteen years of experience in the direct selling business. My intention is to empower you to make a sound decision. Ultimately, the decision will be yours and I am sure you will make a wise one.

Direct Selling—International and Indian Scenario

It is believed that the direct selling industry was born sometime in the 1930s or '40s in USA. Gradually, it spread its wings across the globe owing to its widely popular values and benefits, and has been growing consistently ever since. As per the WFDSA Annual Report 2019 (World Federation of Direct Selling Associations, USA, established in 1978), global direct selling industry sales stood at US$192.9 billion in the year 2018. 79 per cent of the global sales have been generated by the top 10 countries and 24 countries have posted sales of more than US$1 billion each.

Individual sales of the top 10 countries have been shown in the figure below:

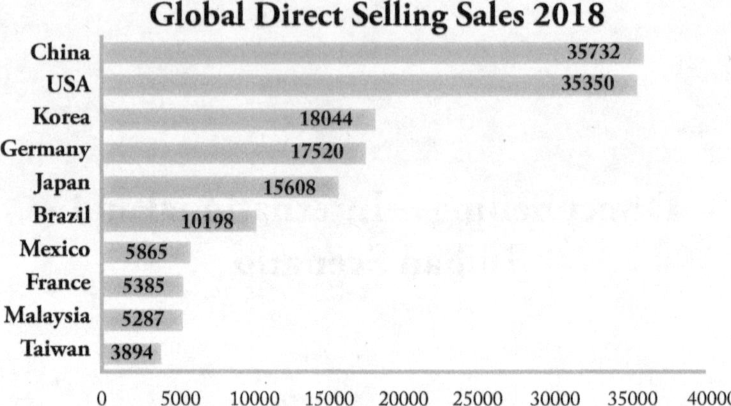

As per the same report, 118.4 million people have been associated with direct selling globally in the year 2018, and this number has been growing consistently.

As far as India is concerned, direct selling came here in the 1990s. The industry kept growing at a steady pace in spite of several challenges. Several illegal pyramid schemes also mushroomed to reap the benefits of an expanding industry and brought the field a bad name. Many who didn't fully understand the totality and depth of the business promoted it in their own ways.

But over the last few years, several industry bodies and government agencies have worked to create a positive environment and a robust regulatory framework for massive growth of the industry in India. Slowly, people are realizing its immense potential. Constant awareness and guidance is empowering people to build this business the right way and fulfil their dreams.

FICCI has been playing a key role in the same; various reports on the industry can be found on the FICCI website. The government has already issued official guidelines for direct selling in India in September 2016. Since then, the industry has received a big boost. A recent report by FICCI-KPMG projected that retail sales in direct selling could reach ₹ 64,500 crore by 2025 and provide self-employment opportunities to 1.8 crore Indians, 60 per cent of whom are women.

I believe that the industry is ready with huge opportunities for everyone and it's only the beginning of a golden period for direct selling in India.

The Right Way to Start Your Direct Selling Business

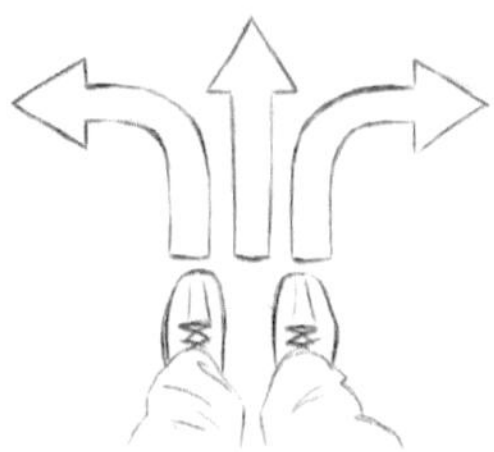

The journey of a thousand miles begins with a single step.

–Lao Tzu

Although the right beginning is important for a business venture, or for any other goal that you want to accomplish in life, it is doubly crucial in direct selling. That is because, in this business, you have not invested any money and there is no office/boss, so quitting at the first sight of a challenge is very common. I believe you should work with these three basic objectives in the first few weeks—understanding, retention, and take-off.

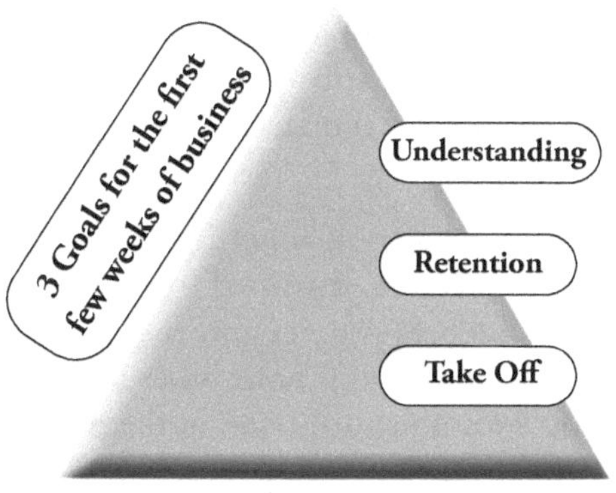

1. **Understanding:** You must understand the basics of the business—product range, income plan, different types of training/events, and different activities required for building the business. The best way to develop understanding is by attending events and counselling with seniors.

2. **Retention:** Mastering anything new takes time. Any change or new activity is difficult in the beginning. Please remember, everyone who is an expert today started out as an amateur. Every teacher was once a student. So commit yourself to the business for at least the next few months. Don't make the mistake of quitting too soon. If this industry has been fulfilling the dreams of millions of people in 179+ countries for so many decades, why will it not work for you?

   Making mistakes is acceptable, but quitting is not right. Don't quit in the face of difficulties or challenges. Close down the business if you don't like its value system and the way it is done, but do so only after understanding it completely. It may be possible that you may have joined the wrong company, the wrong team or a wrong upline; change these if you need to, but don't leave the industry merely because of any initial challenges you face.

   Anytime you feel like quitting, just recall why you started. Give yourself at least three to twelve months, and keep doing all you can in this period under the guidance of your upline and as per the system.

3. **Take-off:** I strongly believe that doing is the best way of learning. I can even say that persisting at practising something is the only way you can really learn and master something. So, as soon as possible, start using the products and start conducting various activities, such as taking appointments, sharing products, sharing business opportunities, attending events, inviting people to events, etc. Your understanding will deepen with every meeting and phone call.

I highly recommend a companion for you in this critical initial phase of starting your business. A trusted friend who can be with you all the time and who will help you not only to survive but also to thrive in the business. This companion is none other than the #1 bestselling, most read and most recommended book in the direct selling/network marketing industry—*Be A Network Marketing Millionaire*.

I am recommending it not simply because it's my book, but for its powerful content. 12 years of wisdom gained from working with more 7 lakh people has been condensed in this one book. Whichever company you choose to work with, the principles, ideas, strategies and tolls included in this book will give excellent results with every company, plan and product. Just check the Contents page and you will realize that every single possible question on direct selling/network marketing has been answered in this book. This is one book that is enough to ensure success in direct selling.

Your business doesn't start the day you register or buy some products. Count your starting date as the day you have faith in the business, understanding what it takes to go to the top, the day you start conducting your meetings. Only once you have done 30 one-to-one meetings and attended at least 10 training events, will I consider that you have really started the business.

Don't start full-time. Don't test the depth of the water with both feet right away. I don't know if you will be able to perform in this business. Try it. If you cannot build a good business part-time, you cannot build a big business full-time. Master it. Once you are ready for it, then take up this business full-time.

Why People Fail in Direct Selling

You may ask: *If there are so many good things about direct selling and so much support is available, then why do so many people fail in this business?*

I believe direct selling is like any other business. So people fail here for the same reasons why they fail in any other business or work in life. Yet, there are a few things that are unique about this business, and a quick discussion will give you the right perspective. The points listed below will also throw some light on why many people talk negatively about this business.

Although I am answering this question here, please be aware that most of the so-called failures in direct selling are those who have not even opened their product packs, or not attended even one basic training. Many don't even know the complete details of their products and income plan. These people are willing to wait joyfully and proudly for a few years to make their first profit in any other traditional business, but they begin calling direct selling business a failure without even putting in a few dedicated hours first.

Moreover, for someone to fail, they need to start something. Buying products or just attending a meeting is not called starting a business. Most people who say that the business doesn't work are the ones who didn't put in even six to ten hours of serious work. With my hands-on experience of thirteen years of direct selling, I have understood some of the common reasons why people fail in the business. These are:

1. **People underestimate this business:** Most people are not able to envision what all this business can do in their lives. Many don't even look at it like a business. I find it really tragic that people quit the business without even fully realizing what it could have done for them. When they underestimate it, they don't put in the efforts required and, naturally, they do not get the desired results. Then they quit altogether, further strengthening their belief that this is not really a business at all!

2. **Starting with wrong expectations:** Many people come into this business expecting it to be a cakewalk. They feel once they start the business and talk to a few friends, everyone else will start as well and the business will give them ongoing income. People buy products expecting it to be a lottery or a get-rich-quick scheme. Many who take up this business have never done a business before, and they have absolutely no idea of what kind of effort and commitment will be required for any business venture.

   Some of these expectations are general opinions held by people while some others are set wrongly by the person who introduced the business to them. But when they find out that the reality is different from their expectations and they have to work hard for success, they quit the business.

3. **Zero entry cost:** The biggest advantage of this business is also its biggest disadvantage. You don't need any investment, stock, staff, set-up or working capital to start a direct selling business, so anybody can just walk in and call themselves a business owner. This free entry attracts ignorant and non-serious people who later complain, 'This business doesn't work. 'Generally speaking, since they have not invested anything and there is no risk involved, there is no commitment or seriousness in building the business. Since all they have done is shopping for some products, it doesn't feel as if they have started something big that can change their future and the future of further generations.

4. **No accountability:** There is no boss nor any other authority to force you to do the activities required for success; it's purely a self-driven business. Nobody can determine your working hours,

location or working style. Being self-driven is a rare talent, and many people drop out because of lack of self-motivation and accountability.

5. **Zero exit cost:** Since it doesn't cost anything to quit the business, it is really easy for people to leave. Furthermore, you may find that many others in your circle have also quit the business, so you will become a part of the failure party and no one will single you out and label you a failure when you quit.

   Many direct selling companies sell health supplements. Many chemists also sell supplements in the market. If a chemist doesn't make a sale in a day, will he close the shop next day? No. In traditional business, people are ready to wait for years in the hope of making a profit because they have invested a lot of money and made a set-up that will be a total waste once they quit. Add to that the fear that if they shut shop, they will be labelled failures by their relatives and neighbours. Since network marketing doesn't have either of these, people freely quit.

   I would find it very funny when people told me that they have quit the business. I used to ask them, 'You can only quit something that you have started. You have just bought a product and that is not called starting a business in any sense.' Many others engage in it as if it is a weekly or monthly hobby. You don't quit a hobby.

6. **Not willing to follow the system:** Every business or profession has its own set of operating systems and guidelines that must be followed in order to achieve success. Likewise, direct selling has its own set of guidelines and success principles. There are some specific ways to build this business. People approach this business with an attitude of: 'I know how to do it. I have already done it. I understand this, my friend also did this type of business, please don't teach me how to do it.'

   The problem is, first, people don't listen due to their ego or attitude. They try out their own ideas and style. When they face a setback, they quit the business saying, 'I knew it from the beginning, these businesses don't work... Nobody is willing to start this business... This is why people are negative about this business...' and so on. The tragedy is—to be a doctor, you are ready to learn for so many years. To be an engineer or a CA, you are willing to spend time and money for so many years. But to be a successful direct seller, a profession that can give you unlimited income, freedom and a dream lifestyle, you are not willing to learn even for a few days.

It's a classic case of little knowledge being a dangerous thing. Not only here but in every other profession, this same rule will be applicable. It's just that in other professions, people have accepted the wisdom of that saying, while here, they may take some more time.

7. **Lack of focus and time:** Direct selling is a part-time business for a majority. They have a primary job/profession or business, and they start direct selling in an attempt to build a second income source. So, people are already facing immense pressure in their current job/profession. They are struggling to achieve a work-life balance. On top of it, however desperately they need a second income, people are living in a comfort zone adjusting with their current income and lifestyle.

   Since so much is already happening in their life, most entrants in this business are not able to give it their focus and time. They keep waiting for a day when they will be free to give some time to this business, and this wait slowly drowns their initial excitement and they quit.

8. **Working with myths:** Many people start this business with a few myths or wrong beliefs and that thwarts their success.

   'I know everything about this business.' Trust me, 90 per cent of those who failed in this business thought they knew everything about it. If someone already knew everything before they began, they would have risen to the top and not failed. After thirteen, full-time, active years in the business, I believe I still need to learn a lot more about this business. This myth is a life-breaker.

   'This business is very tough to do.' I felt the same too in my initial years in the business. But, gradually, I realized that nothing is easy or difficult. Let me give you some simple examples. The strap of my wrist watch breaks and I try to fix it. It's tough for me, but for a watch mechanic, it will take less than a minute and the person may not even charge money for this. My wife loves to cook for me, and when she makes wheat roti (bread) for me, every roti is equally round and puffy. But imagine if I start making rotis, every one of them will look like the map of a different state and God knows what disaster may happen in the kitchen! Roti-making is tough for me but easy for my wife. This rule holds true for everything in life—Nothing is easy or difficult, whatever you decide to learn and practise becomes easy for you over a period of time.

For some people, riding a bicycle is tough, and there are some others who easily drive airplanes and space ships. Whatever you are doing easily right now was tough once upon a time. It has become easy for you with your commitment to practise it consistently. Direct selling, too, will become easy for you with continuous practice.

'There is no respect in this business.' Many people live in the illusion that the profession they choose determines the respect and success they get. Show me one profession where everyone is respected. There are doctors who are respected and doctors who are hated. There are spiritual gurus who are respected and there are gurus behind bars. There are respected CAs, lawyers, engineers, among other professionals, and there are millions of them who are unknown and struggling for survival. Many of them are even considered cheats. What I have learnt in life is this: Your profession doesn't give you respect or success; rather, it is the commitment, honesty and ethics with which you conduct that profession that determines the level of respect, admiration and financial success you receive. Of course, when I make this statement, I am only talking about businesses that are legal and ethical in every sense. So choosing the right company and the right mentor is important.

'How can this business give so much money?' This business can give you as much money as any other business. The type of business doesn't determine the amount of money you earn; the volume/turnover decides the amount of money you earn. If you start a business and don't produce any sales, you will not get any income. Income in this business is determined purely by the volume you and your team generate, and this is exactly how it works in any other business. There is a fixed percentage of income that is given to everyone, and whoever generates more volume gets a bigger income. It's that simple.

'I am not good at selling.' Many people avoid starting a direct selling business because they believe they are not good at selling. They believe a direct selling business is all about selling products or services. This field works on sharing and recommendation, and sharing is basic human nature. The key to success in this business is nurturing relationships, empowering people, developing leadership and building a community of like-minded people. Moreover, you will be trained by your seniors on all the selling and communication skills required. What we don't realize is that everybody is selling all the time, anyway. If you are afraid of selling, I recommend you read the special chapter on the selling mindset in the book, *Be A Network Marketing Millionaire.* Let's solve this puzzle called selling.

In fact, I have seen innumerable sales people who were miserable failures in direct selling. The reason is they were too good in selling and nobody could duplicate them. The key in this business is not your selling skills, but doing things that are duplicable. I deeply instil this belief in people when they come for my direct selling training event: 'We don't do great things in direct selling; we do what is duplicable.' Furthermore, for salespeople, closing a sale is the end of their work, but in direct selling, closing a sale is just the beginning of the work.

On similar lines, I have seen many people who were excellent stage performers but couldn't build a big direct selling business. I am not saying that people with good selling or public speaking skills will not be successful in this business; I am only saying that these are not the primary qualities required for building a big direct selling business.

If there is anything else on direct selling that you want to understand in depth, just refer to my #1 bestselling book—*Be A Network Marketing Millionaire.*

5-Minute Exercise for You

Knowledge is a dormant power; for it to become a real power, it must be used and applied. You can apply something only if you have learnt it well, and repetition is the best way to learn anything.

For the next five minutes, I urge you to quickly write down the five best things that you have learnt about direct selling after reading this book. You may even write down what you loved in this book, or some of your old opinions that have changed after reading it. You need not go back to the book and write down the exact words. Write whatever comes to your mind instantly. You are doing this exercise only for yourself. You can also do this exercise in your notebook. In fact, you can follow this practice for every book you read.

1. ____
   ____
   ____

2. ____
   ____
   ____

3. ____

4. ____

5. ____

The Next Steps

A real decision is measured by the fact that you have taken a new action. If there is no action, you haven't truly decided.

–Tony Robbins

Thank you so much for reading this book. I must appreciate you for reading the entire book and reaching this page. It clearly shows your quest to learn and grow. Kudos to you.

Sharing is caring. If you loved this book, please share it with as many people as you can—your family, friends, teammates, prospects, and anyone you care about. You can even lend this book to your prospects before you go to share your business/products, I am sure when you go to pick up your book, they will be more positive and open to your meeting.

I would really appreciate it if you could share your valuable feedback on this book, and on any other work of ours that you have come across. Your suggestions on anything that you want me to add or change in this book or any other of our books, videos, etc., are welcome.

If you want to pursue a direct selling business and if you have any question whatsoever regarding this business, I can highly recommend reading the book—*Be A Network Marketing Millionaire.* At the time of publication of this book, it is available in 6 languages wherever good books are sold. This one book has everything you need to know about this business. It's an excellent read even for people who are not into direct selling. It has invaluable lessons to offer on entrepreneurship, sales, leadership, teamwork, relationships, and success in life.

We have one of the largest training resources on earth for network marketing/direct selling—online courses, free video trainings, free e-books, live workshops, books, high-performance coaching, and much more.

Also remember to work only with the right mentor and the right company.

Looking forward to helping you and serving you in building your dreams.

Your partner in success,

Deepak Bajaj

Feedback/queries – info@deepakbajaj.biz; www.deepakbajaj.biz

Deepak Bajaj's Life Changing Tools and Solutions

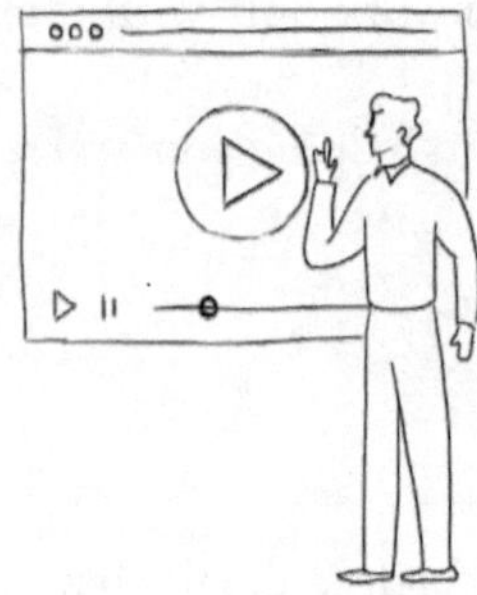

There is no secret to success; there is always a system to success.

–Deepak Bajaj

For almost two decades, I have been passionately obsessed with creating tools for empowering people to accomplish their dreams easier and faster. In fact, this is my life's mission. My books, talks, videos, online courses, workshops, and everything else I do are centred on this mission. I strongly believe each one of us has seeds of greatness inside us. We all are ready and deserve a life of success, happiness, bliss and abundance. Along with my partners and my team, I want to contribute in your journey to success, happiness and abundance through our research-based, constantly evolving and proven tools and solutions.

All my tools and trainings have been designed with one clear goal—it should bring about instant change and lasting transformation. Transformation is possible only through upgradation of knowledge, skills, mindset and emotional quotient. This is possible only through right education and tools, and not simply motivation. Motivation is temporary; skills and transformation are permanent. Team Deepak Bajaj has one of the biggest ranges of resources available for success in direct selling and any other area in life. You can get all updated details on our website www.deepakbajaj.biz

But here is a glimpse of all major tools and solutions:

1. **Free Video Trainings** – Deepak's YouTube Channel is considered one of the most transformative and biggest free training resources available online. It has a big collection of life-changing videos full of knowledge, tools, ideas and techniques to take you to the next level. You can find videos on direct selling/network marketing, relationships, teambuilding, success, goals, leadership, public speaking, communication, and many other subjects at www.youtube.com/deepakbajaj
2. **Online Courses** – You can master the best international knowledge, tools, skills and ideas right from the comfort of your home with our online courses. These courses have unique methodology and style that bring you the desired results from every programme.
3. **Books** – What you are holding in your hand is the second book by Deepak Bajaj. His first book has been on bestseller charts since its launch in June 2018 and has been among the most read and most followed books in the direct selling industry. This book—*Be A Network Marketing Millionaire*—is a must read for anyone who wants to achieve success in the direct selling industry. We also have some powerful e-books which you can download from our website www.deepakbajaj.biz totally free of cost.
4. **Live Workshops** – Deepak's workshops are famous for their incredible energy and real-life transformation tools and techniques. Deepak has already trained and coached more than 7 lakh people. These workshops always run houseful thanks to their unique methodology, result-delivering activities, best international course material, and transformative tools and techniques.
5. **Social Media** – You can access a host of valuable knowledge, tools, ideas and techniques free of charge by following Deepak Bajaj on various social media platforms, including YouTube, Instagram, Facebook, LinkedIn, TikTok, etc.
6. **High Performance Coaching** – For those who want to

achieve nothing but the best, that too at jet speed, there is a high-performance coaching programme where Deepak will personally work with you with customized solutions to take you or your organization to the next levels of excellence in whatever you choose—health, happiness, profitability, business multiplication, emotional challenges, among other areas.

7. **Speeches** – Deepak has been regularly invited by corporates, universities, government organizations and different independent bodies to deliver his electrifying and transformative speeches that not only motivate the audience but also produce the desired results. These speeches are generally of a duration of 30 minutes to 2 hours, and are customized to the client's needs. Deepak works with a unique 6-component formula to deliver transformation in every speech.
8. **Customized Training** – Deepak and his team conduct customized training sessions on a variety of subjects for corporates, universities, government organizations and different independent bodies. Deepak's corporate experience, international NLP certification and 16 years of training experience with more than 7 lakh people brings about instant change and lasting transformation for every training he conducts.

Get all the necessary information at: www.deepakbajaj.biz

Gratitude

My sincere gratitude to each and every one of my readers, network marketing associates, YouTube subscribers, social media followers, workshop participants, coaching clients, teammates, and everyone of you who have touched my life with your presence and wisdom. Every interaction with you has deeply impacted me and made me the person I am. You have been bestowing upon me ever-growing love, support and prayers. What you all have done to me and for me has been invaluable and I can never thank you enough for that. This book is me, and you have made me. This book is all yours. Thanks a lot.

Behind everything I do, I have an incredible 24 x 7 support system—my family. I am lucky to have found all of these in my family—best friends, companions, partners, advisors, cheerleaders and my biggest supporters. I am nothing without all the love, care, support, affection and inspiration you all give me. Thank you Papa, Mamma, Tanima, Gaurav, Divya, Devanshi, Cheeraayu, Prashansa, Nirbhay and Saksham.

My sincere gratitude to my brother and business partner, Gaurav Bajaj. He is the moving force behind the massive success of our business. He is the backbone behind all our achievements. I believe he is the best direct selling leader on earth.

www.ingramcontent.com/pod-product-compliance
Lightning Source LLC
LaVergne TN
LVHW090520110826
845146LV00003B/938

* 9 7 8 9 3 8 9 6 4 7 3 5 8 *